D1055814

The Power OF Positive Habits

Put Your Mind and Body on Autopilot
in 21 Days and Reach Your Goals Automatically!

Dan Robey

Abritt Publishing Group
Miami, Florida
www.abritt.com

The Power of Positive Habits

by Dan Robey

Published by:
Abritt Publishing Group
P.O. Box 77-1148
Miami, Fl 33177-1148 U.S.A.
orders@abritt.com

www.thepowerofpositivehabits.com

All rights reserved. No part of this book may be reproduced or transmitted in any form or by any means, electronic or mechanical, including photocopying, recording or by any information storage and retrieval system, without written permission from the author, except for the inclusion of brief quotations in a review.

Every effort has been made to ensure that the information that is contained in this book is accurate and complete, we assume no responsibility for errors, omissions or inaccuracies. Therefore, you should use this book as a general guide only. Neither the author nor the publisher are engaged in rendering any professional services or advice to the individual reader. The suggestions, ideas and procedures contained in this book should not be intended as a substitute for consulting with a physician or professional advisor. The reader is advised to consult with a physician before beginning any exercise or diet program. Neither the publisher or the author shall be liable or responsible for any loss, damage or injury allegedly arising from any suggestion or information contained in this book.

Unattributed quotations are by Dan Robey

Copyright © 2003 by Dan Robey, All Rights Reserved

ISBN, print, ed.   0-9725219-7-6

Library of Congress Control Number: 2002114925

Cover Design by Andrew Newman

Interior Design by Tammy Grimes

ATTENTION: ASSOCIATIONS, MANUFACTURERS, EDUCATIONAL INSTITUTIONS, INDUSTRY PUBLICATIONS, ORGANIZATIONS. Quantity discounts are available for bulk purchases of this book for subscription incentives, premiums, reselling, educational purposes, fund raising, gifts. Custom versions of this book can be created to fit specific needs. For more information please contact Bill Edwards, Special Sales Department at Abritt Publishing Group P.O. Box 77-1148, Miami, Fl 33177-1148 U.S.A. Tel. 305-238-1356. E-mail bill@abritt.com

To my father, Gerald Eugene Robey,

who has always encouraged me to pursue my dreams,

and to my mother, Martha Lou Robey... it's another beautiful day mom.

Contents

Chapter 4 119

Acknowledgements

First I would like to thank everyone at the Abritt Publishing Group, their dedicated efforts helped make this book a reality. A heartfelt thanks to my editor Marilyn Power Scott, without your enthusiasm, creative ideas, suggestions, and of course excellent editing skills, this book would not have been possible.

Special thanks to my cover designer, Andrew Newman, an extremely talented individual who put up with my many requests for design changes and who also assisted with interior design modifications. Thanks to Carolyn Porter for excellent editing work during the first phase of book production. I would also like to thank Tammy Grimes for the terrific interior design and Lynn Grimes for your great proofreading work.

To my readers panel who took the time to digest and analyze the first drafts of the book and provide valuable suggestions: Eileen Gilbert, you gave me inspiration during the times when I needed it the most. I can't thank you enough. Wendy Russell, Peter Bernath, Vijo Mennon, Bob Bonnen, Brenda Simmons, Tom and Sharon Sanders, thanks for your suggestions and encouragement. To my lifelong friend, John Russell, thank you for always being there to remind me, "It's not about us, it's about God."

To my beautiful wife Pamela and my daughter Brittany, you are the motivation for everything I do.

A special thanks to an incredible group of experts, whose years of dedicated research in the fields of health and nutrition, fitness, and medicine, provided the science behind many of the positive habits in this book: Dr. Joann Manson, Chief of Preventive Medicine at Brigham and Womens Hospital – Professor of Medicine at Harvard Medical School; John Acquaviva, Ph.D., Assistant Professor of Health and Human Performance at Roanoke College; Bill Hebson, President of Hebson Fitness Centers, Stuart, Florida; Dr. Margo Denke, University of Texas Southwestern Medical Center; Teh Kong Chuan of the Singapore Sports Council; Dr. Bryant Stamford head of Heart Promotions and Wellness Center at the University of Louisville; Christine Clark, Ph.D., director of sports nutrition at Penn State University; Joseph Kasof, Ph.D., University of California, Irvine; John Kirwan of the Noll Physiological Research Center at Pennsylvania State University; Larry Scherwitz, Ph.D., University of California; Loreli Disogra RD, The National Cancer Institute; Dr. Sam Bhathena, Phytonutrients Laboratory of the US department of Agriculture; Dr. Walter Willet, of Harvard University.

To the teachers whose writings and words have shaped my life, and in some cases saved it, over the past thirty years: Napolean Hill, Paul C. Bragg and Patricia Bragg, Zig Ziglar, Norman Vincent Peale, Anthony Robbins, W. Clement Stone, Wayne Dyer, Brian Tracy and Dale Carnegie.

WHAT ARE
Positive Habits
AND WHAT CAN THEY
Do For Me?

Sow an act and you reap a habit.
Sow a habit and you reap a character.
Sow a character and you reap a destiny.
– Charles Reade

Habits Are Powerful Vehicles for Personal Change

Think about the habits you have now and how they affect virtually every aspect of your life. Your weight and health are determined by your eating habits. Your relationships with people are determined by your social habits. Your success at work is determined by your work habits. You have sleeping habits that dictate how well you sleep. You have sexual habits. You even have buying habits; just take a look around your house and you will quickly see them. Our character, health and virtually every aspect of our lives are indeed determined by our habits.

If you ask ten people on the street what the word *habit* means, nine out of ten will tell you that a habit is a negative action that people do over and over again, like smoking, or procrastinating, or eating too much. Bad habits get all the press. Let's look at the results of just one bad habit: smoking. Every year, over 400,000 people lose their lives to smoking-related illnesses in the United States. Imagine then, the negative power that exists in just that one bad habit. It is staggering.

> Our character, health and virtually every aspect of our lives are indeed determined by our habits.

Now I want you to think about an even greater power, a power that can bring you success, health and happiness; a power for positive, permanent, and automatic personal growth: the power of positive habits. Let's look a little closer at the meaning of the word *habit*. Random House dictionary defines *habit* in this way:

> *Habit: An acquired behavior pattern regularly followed until it has become almost involuntary.*

The important words in this definition are *acquired* and *almost involuntary*. Let me ask you a question. When is the last time you sat down and said to yourself, "Today I am going to add a new habit to my lifestyle?" I would venture to guess that you have probably never said those words. As you read this book, you will see how easy it is to add positive habits to your life and the great power they have to change it. Think about the words *almost involuntary*. This means the habit is so powerful in your mind that it is almost unstoppable! With respect to bad habits like smoking, procrastination, and overeating, this is very bad. But with the positive habits you will learn about in this book, this is very, very good.

What is a positive habit? A positive habit is simply a habit that produces positive benefits, actions and attitudes you want to acquire and make a part of your life. Why is there such great power in positive habits to effect change? Because habits, by their very nature, are automatic. After a period of time they can become permanent.

Imagine the power of being able to lose weight automatically and keep it off forever, to be healthier automatically for the rest of your life, to have better relationships with people, to have more success, to effect positive and permanent change to any aspect of your life…automatically. What better program for personal, positive growth could there be than one that is permanent and automatic?

Put Your Mind and Body On Autopilot

Although most of us have been on commercial airliners, few of us think about the process that takes the plane from point A to point B. Before the plane takes off, the pilot first consults his flight plan. The flight plan describes the details of the trip: destination, time of departure, estimated total flight time, altitude, total fuel required, and so on.

The pilot then programs this information into the plane's autopilot computer. This is the data the autopilot computer needs to complete its mission. That's it! With the technology that exists in today's commercial airliners, the pilot can just sit back and relax while monitoring the plane's progress. The plane's autopilot computer system will fly the plane to its destination and even land the plane...automatically.

Throughout *The Power of Positive Habits,* I will refer to the autopilot system. But now the plane is you; the flight plan is the Positive Habit Program you create with the help of this book; the data are the positive habits that provide the fuel to reach your destinations. Like the pilot, you will create a flight plan. You will select your destinations and program the data into your own autopilot system. Most important of all, you will put your mind and body on autopilot to reach your destinations with the help of your newly acquired positive habits.

The Power of Positive Habits is the Flight Plan for Your Life

That is what the Power of Positive Habits Program is all about. It puts your life on autopilot, just like the captain of the jetliner who programs in the course to a destination city. Do you have life destinations? Maybe you have a vision of a more trim, fit and healthy body. That's a destination. Perhaps you want a better relationship with your spouse or lover. Maybe your desire is to be more successful in business. In the Power of Positive Habits Program, they are all destinations.

So sit back and relax. Prepare yourself for a journey. Get excited! Your life is about to change in ways you never imagined! Get ready to program your life destinations. Most important, get ready to reach them and make them forever yours with your own internal autopilot: positive habits.

Habits Are Knowledge in Action

Think for a moment. All of your habits are knowledge in action. You are probably saying, "That's crazy. When I smoke a cigarette, it's just because I want to." "When I brush my teeth every morning, its just a routine." Look a little closer. You will see that you smoked the cigarette because you had the knowledge that it would make you feel calmer. Likewise, you brush your teeth because you have the knowledge that brushing teeth reduces cavities. *The Power of Positive Habits* will empower you with new knowledge – knowledge that when actionized into a positive habit can change your life in dramatic ways .

Here are some terms I will be using throughout this book:

Actionizing — Converting knowledge into action. As an example, when your mother told you that brushing your teeth would prevent cavities, you actionized that knowledge by brushing your teeth every day. Before long that actionized knowledge became a habit.

Acquiring a habit — The process of adding a new positive habit to your life. As you gain knowledge about a positive habit, you make a decision to acquire that habit. You acquire the habit by actionizing the knowledge.

Habit Acquisition Stage — The point when your new habit is permanent and automatic. Researchers have known for many years that the time required to turn a repetitive action into a habit is approximately 21 days. You will use this timetable as the length of days that you must repeat an action in order to make it a permanent positive habit. Once you have reached this plateau, in all likelihood you will have reached the habit acquisition stage. This is where you want to be. You can change your life in only 21 days!

Foundational habits — habits that support all your other habits. Think about how a house is built. First, a concrete foundation is poured and very carefully leveled in preparation for the construction of the rest of the house. If there are any defects in the foundation, the house, the walls, roof trusses, and so on will be in jeopardy. Your positive habits program will be built on two foundational habits that you will learn about in chapter two, visualization and one-minute tracking.

Primary habits — Habits that specifically target your life destinations. Because every person is different, every person will have a different set of destinations. As you create your positive habits program, you will select primary habits to acquire. I will also recommend several habits that you may want to select as primary.

Support habits — Habits that provide support to a primary habit. Suppose you selected two habits in the healthy heart section as primary. But you see in the relationships section that there are two habits that also have a positive benefit to your heart. These habits are your support habits.

Many of the habits you choose for your program will have multiple benefits. If you choose to acquire Insomnia Habit 50 (Read lightly before bedtime), this habit supports Success Habit 57 (Read 10 pages per night) which can help you achieve your goals regarding wisdom and knowledge.

Thinking habits — Habitual thought patterns. You may not think of your thoughts as being habitual, but on closer examination you will see that you have specific thought patterns that fall into that category. Have you ever met someone who always seems to think negatively? They say things like, "I just know it's going to rain today and ruin our vacation," or, "These pants make me look fat," or "I always get the bad breaks," or "I can feel a cold coming on and I know it's going to be a bad one."

> You can combine positive habits and increase your benefits expotentially.

Children do not start out thinking negatively. Somewhere along the way they acquired the habit. Remember, your habits are not just physical actions, they are also habits of thought. Some of the positive habits in this book are thinking habits – a permanent change in your thought processes.

Quantifiable benefits — Positive results that can be measured. Every positive habit contains within it a quantifiable benefit and in some cases multiple benefits. The law of gravity says that if you drop a hammer, it will fall to the ground. The same is true for your positive habits. You will receive the positive quantifiable benefits associated with that habit.

As you read through the list of positive habits, you will notice that there is a listing of keyword benefits at the bottom of the page for each habit. Later, you will learn how to use these keywords to locate the habits you need to reach your destinations.

Habit triggers — External stimuli that help to trigger a habit action. Habit triggers can be almost anything: a word, music, a time of day, eating, even another positive habit. You will learn how to use habit triggers to activate your positive habits. Habit triggers are also listed for many of the habits.

Habit combinations — You can combine positive habits and increase your benefits expotentially. One positive habit can change your life; imagine how much your life can change when you start acquiring multiple positive habits in combinations!

Here is an example: Suppose your most important destination is to lose weight. You can combine weight loss habits from the health and fitness chapter with goal setting and motivation habits from the success chapter. This combination of new positive habits in your life can be infinitely more powerful than one single powerful habit. Use your imagination, there is no limit to the possible combinations of positive habits you can create. You will see some suggested combinations in the Habit Tips sections.

About the Habits in this Book

The requirements for a positive habit to be listed in this book are really quite simple. It must be an action or thought process that can become a positive habit over time. The action or thought process must result in a quantifiable positive benefit to the person employing it.

There is no requirement that the positive habit be life-changing although many of them are. Some of the habits may seem insignificant to you but may be quite significant to others. Be prepared for surprises! As I researched this book I was totally amazed at the benefits certain habits can provide.

It's Easier to Acquire a New Habit than to Change a Habit You Already Have

By now you are probably saying to yourself, "This all sounds great. I would love to be able to put my life on autopilot, to achieve my health goals, weight-loss goals, success goals, relationship goals and do it all automatically. But adding new positive habits to my life can't be that easy."

Here is the best news! Acquiring new habits *is* easy. You are doing it all the time; you are just not aware of it. Have you ever rented a car? When you got in the car, perhaps you were a little confused. The ignition switch was different, you could not find the volume control for the radio, the turn signals operated differently.

But in just a few minutes, you acquired the knowledge you needed for a new set of driving habits. By the end of your weekend trip, you were already starting to build a foundation for these new driving habits.

But wait! You are just renting the car, so won't your acquisition of these new habits stop when you return the rental car and resume driving your own car? What would have happened if you had purchased the car? It would be only a matter of days until your new driving routine became an acquired habit. It wasn't hard at all, and you hardly had to think about it. You were easily forming new driving habits that would become permanent and automatic.

Was it hard acquiring your new driving habits? Of course not. You were hardly even aware that you were acquiring them, but you were. Do you chew a specific brand of gum everyday? Perhaps you have a special dessert that you love. I know people who have been chewing the same brand of gum every day for over 20 years! Was that habit hard to acquire? Of course not. They simply found a new product that they liked and began buying it every day. Soon it became a new buying habit. Remember this analogy as you progress through this program.

Knowing that the acquisition of new habits is easy gives you a positive edge in moving forward. You know in advance that your success is virtually guaranteed if you stick to the program. Remember that many of the habits you have right now are just routines. So it will be with your new positive habits; they will become routines, too.

How Positive Habits Can Change Your Life

Some people wait all their lives for the outside to change their inside. But it never seems to happen, because change comes from within us first, then the outside becomes different.

– Elliott Goldwag, Ph.D.

Consider the following illustration of how the Power of Positive Habits Program can change your life.

Jill lives in New York. She is 32 years old, single and dedicated to her career in the fashion industry. There are a lot of things that Jill would like to change about her life. Because she has had problems with her weight for most of her life, she has tried every popular diet. None of them seem to work. She loses weight, but the minute she goes off the diet, she quickly regains it.

She loves her work, but sometimes she can't sleep because of the pressures of her job. Although she gets along pretty well with coworkers, some of them think she is difficult to work with.

Jill began her positive habit program by acquiring the foundational habits of visualization, and one-minute tracking. She created her initial program by selecting several primary and three support habits. The primary habits she selected were targeted to the areas that are most important in her life: weight loss, relationships with people and her problems with insomnia.

One of the positive weight-loss habits Jill selected was a calorie reduction habit. Jill drank at least two cola drinks every day at work. She learned in Weight Loss Habit 20 that substituting sparkling water for soda would cut 1960 calories per week, almost 8,000 calories per month from her diet.

She selected other primary positive weight loss, relationship and insomnia habits. Jill knew that once she reached the acquisition stage, the habits she had chosen would become automatic and second nature to her. Jill soon knew that her foundational habits of visualization and one-minute tracking were already starting to work in her life. She was now more focused on what she wanted.

She was able to accurately track her progress in reaching her destinations. She was beginning to see the positive results of the program and knew she was making progress.

She saw herself getting closer and closer to her destinations. Jill is now on autopilot only 2 months into the program. She can feel the changes in her mood. She feels more positive about herself. The goals she visualized are now coming about, and the quantifiable benefits of her primary and secondary habits are being realized every day.

> **Jill senses a feeling of empowerment like none she has ever experienced before.**

Jill's journey has only just begun, yet she can already feel her success coming. She is living a new reality brought about by the positive habits course she plotted for herself. Jill's weight is now in her target range because her positive habits have resulted in a permanent change in her diet and lifestyle. Her relationships with coworkers have improved and she sleeps better. A profound change has occurred and she knows it. Jill senses a feeling of empowerment like none she has ever experienced before.

Bill is a 45-year-old advertising executive. He is married with three children and lives in Chicago. He likes his job and is doing well with his career, but his relationship with his wife has been deteriorating, causing him great stress. Heart problems run in his family, and he has high cholesterol. Bill knows that he must reduce stress in his life, reduce his cholesterol, and take positive steps to have a strong, healthy heart.

He has a clear picture in his mind of his destinations: he wants a better relationship with his wife and he wants to be healthy and strong for his family. Bill starts building his positive habits program by concentrating on healthy heart habits and relationship habits. He knows how important foundational habits are, and he begins his program with them.

After only 3 weeks into the program, he notices a change in his relationship with his wife. One of his new positive habits has had an immediate, noticeable effect. Every week he has made it a habit to leave short notes of love and appreciation to his wife in places she will be likely to see them. He places a Post-it note on the dashboard of her car telling her he loves her.

The next week, a Post-it note is on their bathroom mirror telling her what a wonderful mom she is to their kids. Bill's wife loves the positive notes he has been leaving her. She has always felt that Bill has not appreciated the hard work she does as both a wife and a loving mom. Now she feels appreciated. Bill realizes that just this one simple, little, positive habit has helped his marriage more then anything he has done in years. He is less stressed as a result of the improvement in his relationship with his wife. This is just the beginning.

He is now acquiring other positive relationship habits. He has acquired several health and fitness habits that will bring positive benefits to his heart and overall health. In just 3 weeks, Bill's life has changed in many ways.

■

Positive Habits in a Minute

It only takes one minute to change your life! How is that possible? Because it takes only one minute to gain the knowledge you need to make a decision to acquire a new positive habit. A new positive habit that may be yours for the rest of your life! Think about the compounding benefits you will receive over a long period of time from just one positive habit.

Remember, knowledge is power. Actionized knowledge in the form of a positive habit is amazing power. Bill's relationship with his wife had been deteriorating, but he acquired the knowledge he needed in Relationships Habit 72, leaving notes of love and appreciation to his wife.

In less then one minute, he had the knowledge he needed to make a decision to acquire a new positive habit. Bill also acquired the knowledge for other positive habits related to cholesterol reduction, relationships, and having a healthy heart. The knowledge for each positive habit was acquired in less than one minute.

Actionize a Positive Habit, and Make it Yours Forever!

It took Jill less than one minute to read the words contained in Habit 20. In that short period of time, she obtained the knowledge necessary to make a decision to acquire the new positive habit of substituting sparkling soda water each time she ordered out at a restaurant. She actionized that habit every time she bought groceries: instead of reaching for a six-pack of cola drinks, she reached for a six-pack of sparkling water.

After 21 days, she had acquired her new habit. It was hers forever. Jill's lifestyle had changed forever with the knowledge she gained in less than one minute! The Power of Positive Habits Program contains dozens of one minute habits. Remember that it only takes one minute to make positive changes to your life.

Your life can change automatically, permanently, and quickly. The lifestyle change you are seeking is just around the corner. So now you are on your way; the weight loss you wanted will come to you automatically. Your relationships with people will automatically improve. You are now the pilot programming your life's autopilot for a successful future. You can place your mind on autopilot using the principles outlined in *The Power of Positive Habits*. Once you have programmed in the data, you will soon reach your destination.

Because habits are knowledge in action, *The Power of Positive Habits* is an action-oriented book. There are many readers who prefer to skip around rather then reading a book from beginning to end. While it is possible to read this book in that way and still achieve a certain level of success, your overall success with this program will be greatly enhanced if you read through chapters one and two before proceeding to create your positive habits program.

■

How to Get the Most Out of this Book

We are what we repeatedly do;
excellence, then, is not an act but a habit.
– Aristotle

This is not the type of book that you read once. You will get the most benefit from it if you use it as reference book. The goals of this book are:

❑ To change the way you think about your habits for the rest of your life
❑ To provide you with the knowledge you need to make decisions to acquire new positive habits and make them a part of your life
❑ To provide you with a simple, easy-to-follow program to assist you in acquiring your new positive habits

You will quickly learn that habit acquisition is best undertaken in small steps. You don't want to overwhelm your mind and body with too many new positive habits at once. Use this book as a reference for increasing your repertoire of habits. Also make sure to use our interactive Web site www.thepowerofpositivehabits.com as a valuable resource. This web site will provide you with:

- ❑ New positive habits as they are added to the program
- ❑ Success stories from others who are using the program
- ❑ A library of forms and research information
- ❑ Links to recommended articles, books, and other reference material
- ❑ Positive Habits Newsletter

You will find a resource section at the end of the book and a suggested reading list. I encourage you to further enlighten yourself by reading the books that relate to the subject areas that are most important to you. I hope that you will stay in touch with me to share your success stories. I can be reached by E-mail at dan@thepowerofpositivehabits.com

I have always wanted to be somebody,
but I should have been more specific.
– Lily Tomlin

I want to emphasize to you that the most important benefit you will receive from the Power of Positive Habits Program is the change in the way you think about your habits and how they affect your life. This change in thinking will have a dramatic effect on your life; I know from personal experience. I am now constantly aware of the habits I have and the new habits I am acquiring; I am also aware of the benefits I am receiving.

Positive habits are now second nature to me and I am always looking for new positive habits that can bring even more benefits to my life and yours. If I have done my job well, you should experience a paradigm shift in how you think about your habits. You will no longer think of them as being a bad thing but rather as an incredibly powerful vehicle for positive change. This shift in thinking will bring with it many benefits, including:

- ❑ Increased self-esteem
- ❑ A more positive attitude about your future
- ❑ A feeling that you are more in control of your life
- ❑ The ability to accurately see where you were and where you are going
- ❑ Improved goal-setting abilities

While researching this book, I interviewed leading experts in the fields of health and nutrition, physical fitness, science, and medicine. I researched books, periodicals, and scientific studies, searching for valuable information that could be distilled into a positive habit. The knowledge now available to you is the result of many years of hard work by some of the world's greatest minds.

Think about the power that you know hold in your hands! You can now actionize that knowledge into positive habits that will help you reach your life destinations.

Knowledge, When Actionized into a Positive Habit, Can Change Your Life in Dramatic Ways!

It is impossible to list in one book all of the positive habits that exist in the world today; tomorrow will bring new positive habits that none of us ever thought of. I have tried to cover the most important positive habits in this first edition of *The Power of Positive Habits*. Yet this is an interactive program and it will be evolving and growing as time goes by.

Conclusion

Let's review what you have learned so far about positive habits and how they can change your life:

- ❑ Virtually every aspect of your life is affected by your habits.

- ❑ Positive habits are powerful vehicles for automatic and permanent change.

- ❑ Habits are simply knowledge in action; actionized knowledge can become a positive habit.

- ❑ It is easy to acquire new habits; you are doing it all the time.

- ❑ It only takes one minute to gain the knowledge necessary to acquire a new positive habit.

- ❑ Once you have actionized knowledge for 21 days, it is likely to become a permanent, positive habit.

In Chapter 2 you will learn how to create your first positive habits program...your flight plan.

OK!
PUT ME ON
Autopilot!

Our power does not lie in our ability
to remake the world, but rather in
our ability to remake ourselves.
– Gandhi

Creating Your Flight Plan

"Flight 37 Leaving for San Francisco at 2 PM"

The longest journey starts with just one step.
– Tao Te Ching

Now that you know what the Power of Positive Habits Program can do for you, it is time to begin programming your own autopilot computer. To create your flight plan, you must know your itinerary. What are your destinations? Where do you want your autopilot to take you? Remember, you can't hit a target if you don't have one. In the beginning, don't overwhelm your mind and body with too many new positive habits. Start out with just one target destination.

The Positive Habits Index

The Positive Habits Index is located in the back of the book, it is a powerful tool that provides a quick and easy way to locate positive habits by their benefits. Many of the positive habits in this book have multiple benefits, so they can only be loosely categorized. As an example, the section on healthy heart habits provides a listing of habits that provide benefits to help you have a healthier heart. While you may be tempted to just look for habits by section, the only way to locate all the habits that target your destination is to use the Positive Habits Index. If lowering your cholesterol is one of your destinations, look in the index for the benefit keywords, *lower cholesterol*. The index will list every positive habit that has *lower cholesterol* as a benefit. Think of the Positive Habits Index as a map to help guide you to your destinations. Here are a few examples:

Destination 1   I want a trim and fit body.

Destination 2   I want to lower my cholesterol.

Destination 3   I want to improve my relationship with
my wife.

Look through the Positive Habits Index and locate the benefit keywords that are associated with your destination. If you want a healthy heart, look up the benefit keywords *healthy heart*; for a trim and fit body, look up the keywords, *get trim and fit*. You get the picture. Then, look up the habits listed in the index. Read the text of each habit and choose the habits that will become your primary habits. Primary habits are the ones that provide the most benefits to help you reach your destination. I have recommended a number of habits that I think you should consider as primary habits; they are marked with a triangle icon ◆.

Now choose your support habits. Make a few photocopies of the form on the next page. (Do not write in the book; leave it blank so you can make copies.) Fill in your first destination in the photocopy of the form, then fill in your primary and support positive habits. If you have access to the Internet, you may download full-sized flight plan forms at www.thepowerofpositivehabits.com.

Flight Plan Form
Make photocopies of this form

Destination		Date Started
Primary Habit #1		
Benefits		
Support Habit #1		
Benefits		
Support Habit #2		
Benefits		

Foundational Habit 1
Positive Visualization

One single idea may have greater weight than the labor
of all the men, animals and engines for a century.
– Ralph Waldo Emerson

After programming your autopilot computer to target your destination, the next step is to acquire your first overall foundational habit: *positive visualization*, the granddaddy of all positive habits. This foundational habit can be summarized in one statement: "We were created in the image of our creator, therefore we are creators." Think about this statement very carefully. Everything you or anyone else has ever done since the beginning of time, began first with a thought. Your thoughts have amazing power to create and re-create who you are.

The positive visualization habit is based upon the principle that we tend to become exactly what we imagine ourselves to be. Scientists have now substantiated the mind-body connection. In his best selling book, *Quantum Healing*, author Deepak Chopra, M.D., says, "As you see it right now, your body is the physical picture, in 3-D, of what you are thinking." Your thoughts can invoke an instantaneous physical reaction in your body. Have you ever been frightened? If so, then perhaps you experienced dry mouth or a queasy feeling in your stomach. This is an example of the instantaneous mind-body connection. It is not only your body that is affected by positive visualization; your entire life can be changed by the foundational habit of positive visualization.

Norman Vincent Peal illustrates this very well in his best-selling book, *Positive Imaging*. He describes a young boy who happened to be walking by a newspaper publishing office. He stopped and peered through the window and was amazed at the activity he saw in the office. The activity that surrounded one man in the office especially interested him. It was the chief editor of the newspaper. The young boy watched in amazement as the editor barked orders to the employees around him.

The boy sensed the power that the chief editor possessed – how the entire newspaper enterprise seemed to revolve around him. The young boy began to visualize himself as that editor. Every day he pictured himself as the editor of that newspaper; he dreamed about it at night. He created a detailed vision in his mind of himself in that editor's chair. He re-created that vision in his mind day after day. Who was that young boy? His name was Roger Ferger. Not only did he become the editor of a large newspaper, he eventually went on to become the owner and publisher of the *Cincinnati Inquirer*, one of the largest newspapers in the country today.

He re-created that vision in his mind day after day.

After Arnold Schwartzeneggar succeeded in his career as a body-builder, he decided that he was going to be the biggest box office star in the world as well. This was quite a goal considering that he had very little acting experience at the time. Within a few years of the release of the blockbuster *Terminator 2*, he had indeed become the biggest box office star in the world. Arnold describes how he uses positive visualization in his life: "What you do is create a vision of who you want to be, and then live into that picture as if it were already true."

Think about the last part of that statement: as if it were already true. This is very important. Once you begin believing your positive visualization in your heart, it becomes a part of your core being. It is burned into your subconscious mind; your conscious and unconscious actions will gravitate toward completion of the picture you have created of yourself. It is also important to note that Dr. Peale says that the power of visualization, or, as he calls it, imaging, is made even more powerful when backed by faith and prayer. Positive visualization is the first foundational habit and the secret to reaching all of your life destinations.

When you go to sleep each night, take a few minutes to visualize the new *you* – what you want to be, the destination you want to reach. Create a movie in your mind and make it as detailed and vivid as possible. Replay this movie every night as you fall to sleep.

❑ Your goal is to create a vision of the new you.

❑ Picture yourself as already reaching the destination you chose in your flight plan.

❑ If you chose a trim and fit body, then picture your body as healthy, trim and physically fit, exactly the way you want it to look.

❑ If a new job or a promotion is your destination, picture yourself as already working in that position. Imagine your every action at your new job, the new office, your new coworkers. The more detail you can put into your vision of the new you, the better.

❑ In addition to the visualization of you reaching
    your destination, picture yourself as happy and
    successful, surrounded by the people who love you.

Play this movie in your mind every night after you lie down in your bed to sleep. Use it as a kind of mental sleeping pill. As you go about each day, do what Arnold did and live into the vision you have created. Remember to repeat this positive habit for a minimum of 21 days.

Benefits

Your entire life is dictated by your thoughts and your habits. Your daily positive habit of visualization will bring you many, many benefits. Here are a few:

❑ Did you know that your skeleton is re-created every 3 months
    and your skin is replaced every month? Your liver is regenerated
    every 6 weeks. Every one of the trillions of cells in your body
    will respond to the positive visualizations you have created
    in your mind; the new you will be created every day as you
    visualize it!

❑ Your vision will become a part of your subconscious thought
    patterns; your actions will gravitate towards completing the
    vision you have created.

❑ Your self-esteem will improve.

❑ You will be more focused on your destinations – and your
    improved focus will help you reach them.

Put a Post-it note on the headboard of your bed with the word Showtime written on it. This will be a reminder to begin playing your movie in your mind as you fall to sleep.

Triggers

If your goal is a trim and fit body, cut out a picture of a model in a magazine whose body you admire. Paste the picture on your bathroom mirror, and every morning, focus on that picture for a moment. Imagine that your body is transforming itself into your vision of the one you see in the picture.

Foundational Habit 2
One-Minute Tracking

Keeping a journal will absolutely change your life
in ways you've never imagined.
– Oprah Winfrey

You are visualizing the new *you* that you want to be. You have chosen a destination that is clear in your mind. Now, track your progress as your internal autopilot takes you closer and closer to your destination. Think of yourself as an air traffic controller. Air traffic controllers know exactly where any plane is at any moment in time; they can tell you what the plane's altitude is, its airspeed, where it has been, and most important, where it is going. Like the air traffic controller, you will track your progress as you approach your destinations by using the foundational habit of one-minute tracking.

What Is One-Minute Tracking?

One-minute tracking is simple. It is an extremely powerful, positive habit that will allow you to quickly track your daily progress toward reaching your destinations. It is amazing how quickly we forget things.

If I asked you to describe detailed information about your health and activities from last Tuesday, chances are you would be hard pressed to remember much. Can you remember what you ate? How many hours of sleep did you get? How much did you weigh on that day? The one-minute tracking habit provides you with a simple journal system for keeping track of your progress. Why is this so important?

How do you feel when you succeed at something? You feel great, right? Nothing will motivate you more and help ensure your total success than the realization in your own mind that you are already succeeding! The foundational one-minute tracking habit will do exactly that. It will change your life by providing you with the air traffic controller's view of your journey.

Here are just a few of the benefits the one-minute tracking habit will provide:

❑ You will have detailed facts about your trip, including the date you started (very important in calculating your 21 day plateau), detailed info on the progress you are making toward reaching your destinations.

❑ When you see positive results as they happen, you will become energized with optimism. Evidence that your new positive habits are delivering quantifiable benefits will motivate you to persevere until your destinations have been reached.

❑ It will remind you that you have reached the 21-day threshold for acquiring a new positive habit.

How to Track Your Progress in One Minute

Keep a simple, short log of your daily positive habit; it's easy, and it usually only takes 1 minute of your time. Each day, make short entries into your tracking log: list such things as your attitude, emotions, diet, weight, responses to situations and conditions in your life. The information you track each day will depend upon the destinations you have chosen.

For example, if having a healthy heart is one of your destinations, you will want to keep track of your cholesterol levels, your blood pressure, your weight. (Obviously, all of this data would not be recorded daily, but some entry would be recorded each day) Try this simple little exercise. Get out a note pad or a sheet of paper and a pencil. Look at your watch. When the second hand hits 12, start timing yourself as you write down the following words:

11/8/02 Fri.–Felt great all day. Started habit 52. Weight 135 pounds. Walked briskly for 20 minutes. Had almonds and nuts for snacks.

Success is yours

when you see

yourself

succeeding!

More then likely, you completed writing down the information in approximately 1 minute. Yet, in that 1 minute, you created an important snapshot of data: your version of the air traffic controller's radar screen. You see where you have been, how fast you are traveling to your destination, and, can estimate when you will arrive. You now have important historical data you can refer to as time goes by, to help you track your progress as you acquire new habits.

Depending on the habits that you have elected to acquire, you will record different types of information. For instance, if you have elected to acquire positive movement habits and positive weight-reduction habits, you will want to record information such as the foods you ate, the positive movements you made (length of times, number of repetitions, etc.).

What you remember about a particular day may be quite different than what actually occurred on that day. Your daily log will allow you to look back over time and see your factual progress, to see exactly how you felt, your weight, your health data (cholesterol levels and blood pressure to name a few). Seeing your progress will reinforce in your mind that the positive habits you have acquired are transforming your life. I know how well this works. For the past 3 years, I have kept a simple, yet informative log of every day of my life. I can tell you exactly how I felt on Wed., July 25, 1999, or any day since.

I can tell you what the results of my exercise programs were, what supplements I took, and how they made me feel on any given day. This log has been invaluable to me as a factual reference of how I reacted to certain events, my weight changes, motivation, attitude and lifestyle. There have been many, many times when I referred to this log to see how I handled a particular situation or the effects of diet changes and supplements that I added to my diet. My activities and daily information are there for me. If I did not keep the log, the valuable information would soon be long forgotten.

It generally takes me less then two minutes to record the log for any day. It is a habit that has become a part of my life; it is now second nature for me. If you have a computer, I recommend typing just three to four lines of descriptive text into a word processing program. An entry might look something like this:

6/21/02 Fri. – felt great all day, did 10 min. on treadmill in am, had protein shake with vitamins, started 30 min. reading habit before bedtime to help my insomnia, slept 7 hours the night before.

The daily log serves many purposes:

❑ It reminds you of your goals and the actions you are taking towards them every day.

❑ It allows you to factually track your progress.

❑ It provides detailed information such as dietary changes, calorie reductions, fat reduction, and so on.

❑ It helps build your self-esteem because you are reaffirming the positive benefits you are achieving through the acquisition of new positive habits.

❑ It helps to paint the picture daily of who you are becoming.

While you will have many successes in life you will also have failures. You can learn from your failures and turn them into opportunities if you can look back and see how you handled them.

I am your constant companion. I am your greatest helper or heaviest burden. I will push you onward and upward, or drag you down to failure. I am completely at your command. Ninety percent of the things you do might just as well be turned over to me, and I will be able to do them quickly and correctly. I am easily managed, show me exactly how you want something done and after a few lessons I will do it automatically. I am the servant of all great people and alas! of all failures as well. I am not a machine, though I work with all the precision of a machine, plus the intelligence of a man. You can run me for profit or run me for ruin - it makes no difference to me. Take me, train me, be firm with me and I will place the world at your feet. Be easy with me and I will destroy you. Who am I? I am Habit.

– Anonymous

Conclusion

Here is a quick review of Chapter 2 and what you have learned about the Positive of Positive Habits Program:

❑ You create a flight plan by defining your destinations and selecting primary and support habits. Your flight plan will take you to your destinations.

❑ Many of the positive habits in this book have multiple benefits

❑ The Positive Habits Index is a powerful tool that will help you quickly locate positive habits by their benefits.

❑ The foundational habit of visualization will help you create the new *you* that you want to be.

❑ The foundational habit of one-minute tracking will help you follow your progress.

In Chapters 3 and 4 you will learn about more positive habits that can change your life. Now it's up to you. Chart your course, your new life awaits you!

Positive Habits

FOR

Health and Fitness

To maintain good health, normal weight and increase the good life of radiant health, joy and happiness, the body must be exercised properly (stretching, walking, jogging, running, biking, swimming, deep breathing, good posture, etc.) and nourished wisely with natural foods.

– Paul C. Bragg

How to Get Trim and Fit Automatically!

Cultivate only the habits that you
are willing should master you.
– Elbert Hubbard

So you want to be trim and fit, and you've tried all the fad diets but
they just don't work. You lose weight at first, but then you put it all back
on and more. Sound familiar? If so, don't feel alone. Millions of people
fail to achieve the trim and fit body they are looking for by dieting alone.
Why? The key to building a permanently trim and fit body is to change
your lifestyle, and nothing can help you change your lifestyle faster then
your positive habits program. Here are just a few of the things you will
learn in this section:

❑ How eating the right fats can actually help you
get a trim and fit body *automatically.*

❑ Positive movement and exercise habits that help you burn
calories and trim fat *automatically.*

❑ Simple eating habits that yield BIG weight loss results.

❑ Positive habits that increase your metabolism
and help you burn more calories *automatically.*

❑ Dining out habits that can help you get lean fast!

❑ Simple exercise habits that are easy to acquire and pack a powerful punch in helping you get a trim and fit body.

Act as if it were impossible to fail.
– Dorothea Brande

Millions of Americans are on the diet roller coaster. They read a new diet book, go on the diet, lose some weight, and then go off the diet and gain it back. Your physique is determined by more then just what you eat. There are many factors that contribute to the way you look:

❑ Your activity levels
❑ Your metabolic rate
❑ Your eating habits
❑ Your drinking habits
❑ Your genes
❑ The types of fat you consume
❑ The amount of calories you consume daily
❑ The amount of calories you burn daily
❑ Your body's percentage of body fat

The key to putting you mind and body on autopilot for a trim and fit body is to change your lifestyle. What is your lifestyle? Two of the basic ingredients that contribute to a person's lifestyle are their routines and their habits. In this part of the program, you will learn how to change both, permanently and automatically.

Your positive habits program will provide you with the lifestyle change you need to reach your goal of a trim and fit body. A permanent and automatic lifestyle change is just around the corner. Remember the rental car story in chapter one?

It was easy acquiring your new habits; you were hardly even aware that you were doing it, but you were. Your life is changing. You are now more aware of your habits. You are actively involved in the acquisition of new positive habits. As a result of your lifestyle change, you will have the body you have been wanting for so long. Remember to refer to the positive habits index to locate all habits that relate to weight loss, fat loss and a trim and fit body.

If You Want Permanent Change, You Have to Change Permanently

Replace Bad Fat With Good Fats

My doctor suggested a
triple bypass...bars, restaurants and bakeries.
– Dean Martin

Some of the most powerful positive habits for a trim and fit body in your arsenal are the positive habits related to replacing bad fats in your diet with good fats. Good fats? Most people only think of fat as being a bad thing. In fact, for many years the media has been promoting "fat-free" diets as a more healthy diet.

Just take a look around your local grocery store; you will see lots of products labeled fat free. Do you think all those fat-free products have resulted in thinner Americans? Think again. The percentage of obese people in this country has been rising every year. Americans are now the fattest people on the planet.

The media has gotten it all wrong. Fat can be your friend! There are certain types of fats that are bad for you. They can increase you risk for heart disease while making you fatter at the same time. Other fats are good for your health and can actually help you burn fat and lose weight! Here are just some of the benefits that the positive fat replacement habits in this chapter will provide to you:

❑ Increase the rate that your body burns fat
❑ Help you lose weight automatically and keep it off

- ❑ Increase your good cholesterol HDL levels and decrease your bad cholesterol LDL levels
- ❑ Help you to curb your appetite and eat less
- ❑ Decrease your risk for heart attack
- ❑ Help balance your insulin levels
- ❑ Help you convert unwanted body fat into energy
- ❑ Help raise your body's metabolic rate (the rate your body burns calories)

The Bad Fats

The fats that are bad for you are saturated fats and trans fats; these are fats that are found in animal products such as butter, cheese, meats, and also in many of the processed foods that we eat. Numerous studies have shown that a diet high in saturated fats may increase blood levels of LDL (bad) cholesterol and total cholesterol, risk factors for heart disease.

Trans fats are the most dangerous dietary fats on the planet. Trans fats are typically produced by applying an artificial process to vegetable oils. These fats are mostly found in fried foods, margarines, and processed foods like potato chips and crackers. Researchers at Harvard University did a study of 85,095 women who had no previous history of heart disease or stroke. During the years that followed, the fifth of the group that had the highest intake of trans fatty acids had a 50% greater risk for heart disease then the fifth that had the lowest intake of trans fatty acids.

A recent study showed that women who ate more then four teaspoons per day of margarine had a 70% higher risk of cardiovascular disease then those women who seldom ate margarine. Despite lobbying by many consumer groups, trans fat is still not listed on nutritional labels.

Some researchers have said that as many as 30,000 deaths per year can be attributed to the consumption of trans fat. Reducing or eliminating trans fats from your diet will help to improve your health and the positive habits that follow will help you do just that.

Simple Diet Changes that Pack a Fat-Fighting Punch

Texas A&M University researchers conducted a study to determine what dietary changes resulted in the biggest reduction in fat. During two different 24-hour periods, they asked 5,649 adults to list dietary changes they made in an effort to reduce fat consumption. The researchers then calculated the changes that resulted in the biggest reduction of fat. Combine these simple eating habits with other weight loss habits, and you will see that trim body in the mirror sooner then you think. Here are the results of the study:

- ❑ Do not add fat to baked or boiled potatoes.
- ❑ Do not eat fried chicken.
- ❑ Do not eat more than two eggs a week.
- ❑ Do not eat red meat.

The *Journal of The American Dietetic Association* also conducted a similar study. Here are their recommendations:

- ❑ Trim fat from meat.
- ❑ Remove skin from chicken.
- ❑ Eat chips infrequently.
- ❑ Avoid putting butter or margarine on bread.
- ❑ Choose low fat cheese over regular cheese.
- ❑ Substitute fruit for fatty desserts.

◆
_____

Habit 3

Take Flax Every Day for a Healthy, Trim Body
and Lower Cholesterol!

_____

Benefits

What is flax?

Flax is a blue-flowering plant known for its oil-rich seed. People have been eating flaxseed since ancient times, it has a pleasant, nutty flavor. The health benefits of flaxseed and flaxseed oil are significant and for that reason this habit is recommended as a primary habit for health and a trim and fit body. Here are some of the benefits of flaxseed and flaxseed oil:

❑ Flaxseed contains both soluble and insoluble fiber. Several studies have shown that flaxseed can help to lower cholesterol in the same way that other soluble fiber foods like oat bran and fruit pectin do. A study at the University of Toronto showed that total cholesterol levels dropped 9% and LDL (the "bad" cholesterol) decreased 18% among a group of women who ate milled flaxseed cooked into bread every day for a period of 4 weeks.

❑ Flaxseed is one of the richest sources of ligans and alpha-linolenic acid. Studies suggest that ligans may help to prevent certain cancers. Flaxseed is one of the few plants in the plant kingdom that provide a high ratio of alpha-linolenic acid (an omega-3 fatty acid) to linoleic (omega-6 fatty acids), it is an excellent source of healthy polyunsaturated fat.

❑ A new study has confirmed that the positive habit
of taking flax seed daily can help you get a trim and fit
body. I interviewed Dr. Sam Bhathena, a researcher at the
Phytonutrients Laboratory of the US department
of Agriculture, he said, "we have observed that flax seed meal
is much more effective in lowering cholesterol then soy. Several
other studies have shown that in general, omega-3 fatty acids,
lower lipid deposition, and help in reducing body weight."

❑ Omega-3 fatty acids — More than half the fat contained in
flaxseed is omega-3 fatty acid type, an essential fatty acid.
There have been numerous studies reporting the health
benefits of consuming omega-3 fats. Recent studies suggest
that omega-3 fatty acids which are abundant in flax seed can
help protect you from coronary artery disease, stroke, high
blood pressure, autoimmune and inflammatory disorders.
Studies on the effects of flax seed on breast cancer are now
under way. Omega-3s can also help boost your metabolism,
helping your body to burn calories faster.

Jorge Cruise author of the best-selling fitness book, *8 Minutes in the
Morning,* is such a great believer in the ability of flax to help you lose
weight, he has developed his own brand of flax seed oil. Flax is available
as raw seed, ground seed and also as an oil which is made by cold pressing
flax seeds. You can purchase raw flax seed, ground flax seed and flax seed
oil at most health food stores. The easiest way to incorporate flax seed
into your diet is to buy ground flax seed meal and add it to your food.

❑ Substitute for cooking oil or shortening in baked goods.
❑ Add ground flax seed to pancakes, waffles and cereals.
❑ Put ground flax seed on salads.

Habit Tips

Here is a great recipe for a super health shake. Make a protein shake with 8 ounces of your favorite juice such as apple or orange, add 2 tablespoons of flax seed oil, 2 tablespoons of soy powder, 1 tablespoon of lecithin, fresh fruit such as bananas, papayas or blueberries. Blend with a hand blender or an electric blender. This power shake will provide you with the health benefits of soy; omega-3's, fiber, antioxidants, and enzymes from the fruit, and the fat loss benefits of lecithin.

Triggers

Flax seed meal is cold processed. You can find it at most health food stores. It is a convenient way of obtaining many of the nutritional benefits of flax seeds, including fiber, magnesium, zinc, ligans and mucilage. Keep a bag of flax seed meal in your refrigerator and a container next to your baking goods. Keep a bottle of flax seed oil handy for protein shakes.

Keywords: Fat Loss, Weight Loss, Healthy Heart, Get Trim and Fit, Live Longer, Lower Cholesterol, More Energy, Lower Cancer Risk, Look Younger, Lower Blood Pressure, Primary

◆

Habit 4

Always Order Salad Dressing on the Side

Benefits

Salad dressing can be one of the biggest sources of fat in a person's diet. Studies have shown that females gets most of their fat from dairy products, margarine, mayonnaise, and salad dressing. By making it a habit to order salad dressing on the side, you can control the amount and type of dressing your put on your salads and reduce the amount of fat and calories that you consume.

Try substituting olive oil or a low fat alternative like balsamic vinegar for bottled dressings. Olive oil contains healthy monosaturated fat and is a key ingredient in the healthy heart Mediterranean diet. Remember that sometimes, small changes in your lifestyle can result in big changes to your life. Every time you eat out, remember to order dressing on the side. After 21 days you will be well on your way to making this a permanent and automatic weight loss positive habit.

Triggers

Your trigger for this habit is the waiter or waitress asking you what type of salad dressing you want on your salad. This is your cue to order the dressing on the side and also to ask for a healthier dressing.

Keywords: Fat Loss, Weight Loss, Healthy Heart, Get Trim and Fit, Live Longer, Lower Cancer Risk, Primary

◆
_____

Habit 5

Substitute Soy Burgers for Hamburgers

_____

Benefits

According to the USDA, Americans eat more beef then any other meat, and a large percentage of that meat comes in the form of hamburgers. The problem is that a typical takeout burger can contain as much as 31 grams of fat, and much of that is saturated fat. A soy burger does not contain fat, it is a great source of protein, and it is also cholesterol free.

A study published in the May 2001 issue of *Cancer Epidemiology Bimarkers and Prevention* showed that for each incremental increase in the intake of soy during adolescence, there was a reduction in the risk of breast cancer. Women who had the highest consumption of soy had only half the risk of women with the lowest intake. In addition, there have been other studies that have shown a reduced risk of colon cancer and prostate cancer with the increased consumption of soy.

Additional benefits of soy protein:

❑ The latest research shows that a diet rich in soy
   is associated with improved breast, colon, and
   prostate health, reduced menstrual disturbances, and
   stronger bones.

_____

❑ The American Heart Association and the FDA recommend that Americans consume more soy protein to help lower their cholesterol and protect their hearts for a longer life.

❑ Soy helps to decrease the amount of fat that your body stores by stabilizing insulin levels.

❑ Soy protein helps to increase your lean muscle mass.

There are many excellent soy burger products on the market; in fact, you can now buy soy burgers at some fast food restaurants. When prepared properly, it is difficult to tell the difference between soy and beef. On a personal note, my wife has prepared chili with soy instead of meat, and our guests never knew!

Triggers

Put soy burger containers in your freezer where you would normally store hamburger meat. You would be surprised at the variety of soy burgers now available in grocery stores and health food stores.

Keywords: Fat Loss, Weight Loss, Healthy Heart, Get Trim and Fit, Lower Cancer Risk, Lower Cholesterol, Build Muscle, Look Younger, Stronger Bones, Stabilize Insulin, Prostate Health, Primary

Habit 6

Always Order Baked Potatoes Plain

Benefits

Potatoes themselves are not fattening; it is what we put on them that makes them so fattening: butter, margarine, sour cream. By always ordering your baked potatoes plain and reducing the amount or changing the type of toppings you put on them, you can reduce your intake of dietary fat.

Some experts estimate that your diet is responsible for at least 40% and as much as 60% of your overall weight management program. Remember, your positive habits will result in a change to your lifestyle. As simple as this habit may sound, it is very powerful when combined with your other positive habits. Here are some tips for non-fat potato topping alternatives:

❑ Non-fat sour cream
❑ Salsa, make that medium or hot
❑ Non-fat plain soy yogurt
❑ Sprinkle of hot pepper sauce like Tabasco
❑ Low-fat Italian salad dressing
❑ Olive Oil

Keywords: Fat Loss, Weight Loss, Get Trim and Fit, Healthy Heart

Habit 7

Eat More Low-Fat Dairy, Lose 70% More Fat, Reduce Cancer Risk

Benefits

Make it a habit to eat more low-fat dairy products like yogurt. A study recently published in the *American Journal Of Clinical Nutrition* reported that women who consumed three servings or more per day of low-fat dairy, like yogurt and skim milk, lost 70% more body fat then women who consumed less then one serving.

This habit can also help to reduce the risk of ovarian cancer. A research study published by the *American Journal of Epidemiology* in 2002, has shown that women who consumed the most dairy products overall, including low-fat yogurt and skim milk, were the least likely to be diagnosed with ovarian cancer, regardless of their ethnic group.

Add fresh blueberries for even more health benefits. Blueberries are loaded with cancer fighting antioxidants. Remember to visualize the fat coming off your body as you eat your yogurt and drink your skim milk.

Triggers

Buy several containers of low-fat yogurt and at least one container of skim milk and keep them on the top shelf of your refrigerator. For the first week, put Post-it notes on them with "Fat Loss Habit" written on them.

Keywords: Fat Loss, Weight Loss, Healthy Heart, Get Trim and Fit, Lower Cancer Risk, Stronger Bones

Habit 8

Substitute Trans-Fat-Free Margarines for Trans-Fat Margarines and Butter

Benefits

Dr. Walter Willet of Harvard University says that trans fat is worse for the heart then saturated fats, he advised choosing margarine low in trans fat rather than butter. "Avoiding trans fatty acids will lower the bad form of cholesterol or LDL," he said, "Also, it can raise the good forms of blood cholesterol HDL, so you get several benefits by avoiding trans fatty acids."

There are now several trans-fat-free margarines on the market, these new trans-fat-free products can help you lower your cholesterol and are better for your heart then trans-fat margarines or butter.

Triggers

Place tubs of trans-fat-free margarines where you would normally keep butter or regular trans-fat margarine.

Keywords: Fat Loss, Weight Loss, Healthy Heart, Get Trim and Fit, Lower Cholesterol

Habit 9

Review Nutritional Labels

Benefits

Make it a habit to review the nutritional labels when you purchase food. Look carefully to see how much saturated fat is contained in each product. Your goal is to reduce the amount of saturated fat that you consume. Try to find more products that have a higher percentage of healthy fats. The fats that are the best for you are monounsaturated and polyunsaturated fats.

Be on the lookout for trans fats, they are not currently labeled. There is a simple way to see if a product has a lot of trans fats. If you see partially hydrogenated oils or hydrogenated oils listed before monounsaturated or polyunsaturated oils, then the product contains a lot of trans fat. Remember, the more you know about the foods that you put in your body, the better.

Triggers

Picking up a product at a grocery store is your trigger to turn it over and inspect the label. Buy a red magic marker and put an X on all the food products in your house that are high in fat. This will remind you to limit your portions of these products.

Keywords: Fat Loss, Weight Loss, Get Trim and Fit, Healthy Heart, Primary

Habit 10

Substitute Peanut or Almond Butter for Butter and Cream Cheese

Benefits

A new study may encourage you to trade in your butter and cream cheese for healthier spreads like peanut butter or almond butter. The study showed that women who exercised in the morning and then ate monosaturated fat and also saturated fat, burned off significantly more of the mono fats than the saturated fats. By substituting good fat spreads for bad fat spreads, you will burn off more fat which will help you reach your goal of a trimmer body.

Triggers

Put peanut butter and almond butter containers where you normally keep butter and cream cheese.

Keywords: Fat Loss, Weight Loss, Healthy Heart, Get Trim and Fit, Lower Cholesterol

Positive Habits
That Move You

He who cannot find time for exercise,
will have to find time for illness.
– Lord Derby

It's actually very simple; if you want a trim and fit body that will be yours forever, you have to move, and you have to move often. Positive movement habits are habits that require movement on your part. They must also expend energy, and in some cases they can also help you to build muscle. You may look at some of them as exercise habits, while others are just habits that help incorporate more movement into your lifestyle.

Bill Hebson is a personal-fitness trainer that I have known for many years. I spoke to him recently regarding the importance of adding movement to your lifestyle and here is what he said: "Real-life activities happen standing. We are rarely if ever asked to apply force in a sitting position or laying down. We live in a dynamic, free weight, three dimensional environment. Your training should stress whole-body multi-dimensional movements, so each exercise trains the most musculature, burns the most calories, elevates the whole body's metabolism, and has the highest transference into real world or athletic abilities. In short, you get the biggest bang for your buck."

What Bill is saying is that you have to incorporate multidimensional movements into your daily life if you want a trim and fit body. Positive movement habits will provide you with an increase in your activity levels and multidimensional movements automatically. How important is movement? Being overweight and physically inactive accounts for more than 300,000 premature deaths annually in the United States, second only to deaths related to smoking. A study done at the University of Texas Southwestern Medical Center at Dallas found that a 50-year-old could be brought back to the fitness levels of a 20-year-old with just 6 months of exercise training!

What Can they Do for Me?

Well for one thing, they can help you reach your goal of a trim and fit body and maintain it permanently. Combine them with other diet and positive movement habits and you have a powerful combination that will get you trim fast. Does that sound good to you? They can also improve your health, make you look younger, and can increase your longevity. Let's see; positive movement habits can help me live longer and while I am living longer I will have a trim and fit body and look younger...not a bad combination, wouldn't you say?

To make daily movement a part of your lifestyle, you simply have to acquire positive movement habits. Once you have acquired them, they will be yours forever and so will the benefits that come with them. They will help you to achieve the trim and fit body you have been wanting and help you to maintain it.

Let's look at the first positive movement habit: brisk walking and its related benefits.

◆

Habit 11

Brisk Walking

Benefits

Not running, not jogging, but walking is your most efficient exercise and the only one you can safely follow all the years of your life.
– Executive Health Organization

Walking as a daily exercise habit can truly be a life-changing positive habit and is one of the most powerful habits for reaching your goal of a healthy trim and fit body. Over the past 20 years, there have been dozens of studies that have proven the benefits of brisk walking.

Thousands upon thousands of people have improved their health and lost weight by the diligent habit of walking. If you think that walking does not provide the same benefits as other more vigorous exercises, think again.

A study published in the September 2002 *New England Journal of Medicine* showed that postmenopausal women who walked regularly lowered their risk for heart disease just as much as women who did more vigorous exercise, such as playing sports or running.

This study suggests that walking is just as good for your heart as heavy exercise. I spoke with study author Dr. JoAnn E. Manson, Chief of Preventive Medicine at Brigham and Womens Hospital, Professor of Medicine, at Harvard Medical School. She said, "The study provides compelling evidence that walking and vigorous exercise provide similar heart benefits, about a 30% to 40% reduction in the risk of cardiovascular disease with 30 minutes per day of either activity."

I also asked her about the benefits of making brisk walking a positive habit, and she responded, "they could surely walk away from heart disease and several other chronic diseases. We have also found that brisk walking for at least 3 hours a week can lower the risk of stroke, type 2 diabetes, and breast cancer. No pain, no gain, is an outdated notion; exercise doesn't need to be strenuous or uncomfortable. It can be easy and enjoyable." Even though the study consisted solely of women, it is likely that men would experience similar benefits from the positive habit of brisk walking.

Here are additional benefits you will receive from your habit of brisk walking:

- ❑ Walking burns calories and helps you lose weight and burn excess body fat.
- ❑ Walking can help to improve your posture.
- ❑ Walking requires no special equipment or gyms.
- ❑ Walking can help lower blood pressure and help prevent circulatory and heart disorders.
- ❑ Brisk, aerobic walking will give you the benefits of other exercises, such as jogging and cycling, but without the risk of injuries.
- ❑ Walking at night can help promote better sleep.

- ❑ Walking increases the amount of oxygen in your bloodstream.
- ❑ Walking helps elevate good levels of cholesterol.
- ❑ Walking can help ease lower back pain.
- ❑ It improves mental performance and mood.
- ❑ It helps build bone strength.
- ❑ It helps reduce anxiety and stress.
- ❑ It Helps to boost your immune system.
- ❑ It slows the aging process.
- ❑ It helps to prevent certain cancers.
- ❑ Walking regularly can help prevent osteoporosis.

Getting Started

It's easy to get started with your walking habit…just walk out your front door and keep going! The best time to walk is in the morning. You are more likely to continue walking on a daily basis as you will have less distractions in the morning. Remember, your goal is to make walking a positive movement habit. In the morning, you are likely to have better control of your time; as the day progresses you are more apt to be interrupted by your daily responsibilities.

With that said, if you cannot walk in the morning, it is better to have a daily walking habit at any time then no walking habit at all. It's best to start your daily walking habit by walking for just 10 minutes. After a few days of walking just 10 minutes, you can increase to 20 minutes and then 30 minutes. Your goal is to acquire a daily positive habit of walking 30 minutes.

Habit Tips

If you prefer using a treadmill, you can burn more fat at about 75% of your maximum heart rate. This is according to researchers at the University of Birmingham in England. You can figure your maximum heart rate by subtracting your age from 220, multiply that by 0.75, and you have your target.

You can dramatically increase the rate that you burn calories by simply putting the treadmill on a 10% incline. As an example, a 145 pound women will burn 300 calories per hour on a level surface at 3.5 miles per hour, but that rate jumps to 500 calories per hour on a 10% incline.

Triggers

Put your walking shoes next to the front door.

Keywords: Fat Loss, Weight Loss, Get Trim and Fit, Healthy Heart, Lower Cholesterol, Look Younger, Live Longer, More Energy, Increased Strength, Lower Blood Pressure, Better Sleep, Improved Self-Esteem, Less Stress, Stronger Bones, Build Muscle, Stronger Immune System, Primary

Habit 12

Wear a Pedometer

Benefits

This is an easy habit to acquire; all you have to do is purchase a pedometer and wear it every time you go for a walk or to work out. This positive habit will help motivate you to keep walking. A pedometer is a small, inexpensive device that you attach to your waist. It senses your body's motion and then counts your footsteps. Pedometers can be a great motivational tool; they have been used in Japan for over 20 years to increase walking.

With a pedometer, you can set goals and see yourself approaching them. Studies have shown that sedentary people who use pedometers and set goals see improvements in their body fat and fitness levels that are comparable to people performing more structured exercises. Remember to record your steps in your one-minute tracking log. Here are some pedometer tips:

❑ Record steps you take while walking your daily routine.

❑ Record daily and weekly activity.

❑ Set a goal of 6,000 to 10,000 steps per day but work up to that goal gradually.

Keywords: Fat Loss, Weight Loss, Get Trim and Fit, More Motivated

◆

Habit 13

Deep Breathing

Benefits

You can live without food for weeks, without water for days, but without oxygen, you will die in a matter of minutes. If you want a healthy body that is full of energy, the habit of deep breathing is the key. The more oxygen you put into your lungs, the more energy you will have. Your body runs on oxygen, and this positive habit will provide your body with more of it.

Breathe From the Diaphragm

Many people have forgotten how to breathe properly. When you watch a baby breathe, you notice that their belly expands with each breath. This is how humans are supposed to breathe, from the diaphragm. The baby's diaphragm is creating a suction that pulls oxygen into the lungs.

As we get older, many of us unconsciously switch from natural deep diaphragm breathing to shallow chest breathing. To experience diaphragmatic breathing, place your hand on your waist. Take a deep breath and expand your belly; your hand should move outward as you inhale and inward as you exhale. If you practice this, you will find that it gets easier and easier to take deep, full breaths from your diaphragm.

Habit Tips

Every time you walk, run, jog, or engage in any physical activity, make it a habit to place your hand on your abdomen and take a few long deep breaths. You will be energized with the added oxygen that the deep breathing brings into your lungs. Start slowly with deep breathing and be careful not to over do it, you may get dizzy.

Triggers

Your trigger is the action of placing your hand on your abdomen.

Keywords: Live Longer, More Energy, Less Stress, Stronger Immune System, Increased Strength, Positive Attitude, Better Sleep, Primary

Habit 14

Jump Rope for Ten Minutes and Get Fit Quick

Benefits

This is a great "get fit quick" habit. Many people say they don't have time to exercise. Your best defense to a packed schedule is to jump rope. Jumping rope is a great way to build stamina and burn calories; in fact, one study said that 10 minutes of jumping rope is equal to 30 minutes of running at a pace of 5.7 mph. Start off slowly and work your way up to 10 minutes a day. Here is some advice to help you get started:

❑ The length of the rope is critical. Stand on the center of the rope with both of your feet together. Hold the ends of the rope up against your sides. The rope handles should come to within a few inches of your armpits.

❑ Warm up first by doing twenty arm circles. Hold the rope handles together with both of your hands and then swing the rope from side to side while bouncing lightly on your feet.

❑ Don't jump too high; jump just high enough that the rope will clear your feet.

Habit Tips

Combine this habit with your positive habit of brisk walking for a powerful trim and fit lifestyle change. Carry your jump rope with you as you walk, and every 10 minutes stop walking and jump for 3 minutes.

Triggers

Leave your jump rope next to your front door so you can't leave the house without being reminded of it, or put the jump rope on top of your television and jump rope while watching your favorite show.

Keywords: Fat Loss, Weight Loss, Healthy Heart, Get Trim and Fit, Live Longer, Stronger Bones, Increased Strength, Build Muscle, More Energy

Habit 15

Reward Yourself to Help Make Working Out a Positive Habit

Benefits

Sometimes you need motivation to make something like working out a positive habit. I spoke with John Acquaviva, Ph.D., Assistant Professor of Health and Human Performance at Roanoke College, regarding rewards. He said, "People want to see a reward...make a deal with yourself, this is fairly effective, make a pact with yourself. If I exercise two days this week, I'm going to take myself out to a nice dinner or I'm going to buy that shirt or the pair of shoes that I want."

He further explained a simple method for reminding yourself of your goals: "What are my goals this week? I'm going to work out Tuesday, Wednesday, Thursday and Friday. Write it down and post it in a place where you can see it, post it on a bathroom mirror or put it on your refrigerator or on your desk at work or even in your calendar." Here are some other tips :

- ❏ Pack your gym bag and place it by the front door.
- ❏ Put your walking shoes or running shoes next to your front door.
- ❏ Leave your workout clothes next to your bedside.

Triggers

Your gym bag and walking/running shoes are obvious triggers. Place them where you will see them in the morning.

Keywords: Fat Loss, Weight Loss, Get Trim and Fit, More Motivated

Habit 16

Run Spot Run! Workout With Your Pet Every Day

Benefits

Need motivation to get up and go every morning? Make it a habit to take your dog for a long, brisk walk every morning. Many people say that this is a great motivator for a morning workout. The best part is that once you make it a daily habit, your dog will never let you forget it!

Habit Tips

Combine this with Habit 12 (wear a pedometer) and keep track of how many steps you and your dog take. A great motivator!

Triggers

Your dog will be the best trigger you ever had! Once you get to the habit acquisition, stage your dog will probably bark at you until you get up and go.

Keywords: Fat Loss, Weight Loss, Get Trim and Fit, More Motivated, Less Stress

Habit 17

Don't Push the Elevator Button!
Lose Weight by Taking the Stairs Every Day

Benefits

Did you know that climbing up an average set of stairs burns 1.8 calories and walking down burns 0.8 calories? Doesn't sound like much? According to Teh Kong Chuan of the Singapore Sports Council, "if you work on the 4th floor and take the stairs up and down 4 times per day, you can burn about 200 calories in a 5 day work week which is equivalent to an hour of brisk walking or half an hour of moderate cycling." Nichole Kerr, a researcher with the Centers for Disease Control says you can lose about 10 pounds during the course of a year if you spend ten minutes a day going up and down stairs.

Remember, habit combining can significantly multiply your results. Add this habit to your other "Trim and Fit" habits and you will soon be on your way to the body of your dreams.

Triggers

Every time you see an elevator, think about turning that ride into a workout by heading for the stairs instead. Look for scenic stairs to climb in city directories.

Keywords: Fat Loss, Weight Loss, Get Trim and Fit

Positive Weight Loss Habits

It's a funny thing about life, if you refuse to accept
anything but the best, you very often get it.
– W. Somerset Maugham

Habit 18

When Dining Out, Control Food Preparation and Lose Weight

Benefits

When you eat out, make it a habit to request how your food is prepared. You should never feel like you have to accept food items exactly as they are described on the menu. Most restaurants will happily prepare your meal in different ways if you just request it. You can ask that they bake or broil fried items. Always remember to ask for salad dressing on the side, (use balsamic vinegar as a fat-free salad dressing) and baked potatoes plain with toppings on the side. According to the *Encyclopedia of Foods: A Guide To Healthy Nutrition*, you can save 10 to 30 grams of fat and 100 to 300 calories per entree.

Think about how this positive habit can help you achieve a trim and fit body automatically! Remember, your new positive habits will result in a change in your lifestyle. The cumulative effects of these lifestyle changes are considerable, they hold the keys to achieving a permanent, trim and fit body.

Triggers

Think of your food servers as your own personal nutrition experts. As they approach your table, imagine that they are coming to give you advice on how to get that trim and fit body you are looking for. How motivated would you be if they actually were nutrition experts?

Keywords: Fat Loss, Weight Loss, Get Trim and Fit, More Motivated, Primary

◆

Habit 19

Eat Four to Five Small Meals Per Day
Instead of Three Large Meals

Benefits

Did you know that large meals increase your body's fat storage? Research done by Dr. Bryant Stamford, the head of Heart Promotions and Wellness Center at the University Of Louisville, showed that 80% of obese people were eating less food then people who had normal weight. The difference is that they consumed all of the food in one meal. Most experts agree that eating several small meals per day will help speed up your metabolism and that will help you lose weight and burn off more fat.

Triggers

Put a Post-it note on your bathroom mirror with "5 meals" written on it.

Keywords: Fat Loss, Weight Loss, Get Trim and Fit, Healthy Heart, More Energy, Primary

Habit 20

Substitute Club Soda or Sparkling Water for Soda Drinks

Benefits

Did you know that carbonated soda drinks are the single biggest source of refined sugars in the American diet? Dietary surveys have shown that soda drinks provide 7 teaspoons of sugar per day to the average American's diet. If you drink two soda drinks per day, you are consuming 1,960 calories per week and over 100,000 calories per year!

By substituting sparkling water or club soda for sugar soda drinks, you can greatly reduce the amount of calories you are consuming. This simple habit can help you achieve a trim and fit body. Here are additional benefits you will receive from this habit:

❏ Healthier teeth: Refined sugar is one of several factors that can help to promote tooth decay.
❏ High-sugar diets may increase the risk of heart disease in people who are insulin resistant.

Triggers

When you eat out, remember to always order sparkling water instead of sugar soda drinks. Add a lemon or lime for additional flavor. Remember, it only takes 21 days to acquire new habits.

Keywords: Fat Loss, Weight Loss, Healthy Heart, Get Trim and Fit, Healthier Teeth, Stabilize Insulin

Habit 21

Drink Green Tea Daily
Burn Fat! Boost Your Metabolism!

Benefits

If you want some help achieving that trim and fit body, make it a positive habit to drink green tea daily. Here are just of few of the benefits you will receive from this positive habit:

The *American Journal of Clinical Nutrition* recently published research demonstrating that a substance found in green tea called catechin polyphenols increases your metabolism and also increases the rate at which your body burns calories. Burning more calories is your ticket to a leaner body.

Green tea is also loaded with antioxidants, which have been shown to protect you from cancer and many other diseases. Other studies have shown that green tea may help you control your appetite.

Triggers

Buy several containers of green tea and keep them next to your other teas.

Keywords: Fat Loss, Weight Loss, Get Trim and Fit, Lower Cancer Risk, More Energy, Healthy Heart

◆

Habit 22

Drink Eight Glasses of Water per Day

Benefits

Most people do not realize how important water is for weight maintenance and overall good health. Christine Clark, Ph.D., director of sports nutrition at Penn State University says, "People don't realize that water is one of the six classes of nutrients." Your body uses water to convert food into energy; it is also used to carry nutrients throughout your body and to regulate body temperature. Through ordinary activity alone, a sedentary person can lose 2.5 quarts of water in a day. When you are exercising, you can lose between .8 and 1.5 quarts per hour. In order to maintain optimum hydration, all of this fluid must be replaced.

By drinking eight glasses of water per day and more when exercising, you will maintain optimum levels of hydration. Dehydration can actually make you look heavier; this is because fluids are held just under your skin. Drinking more water each day is also good for your heart. A study by Loma Linda University showed that men who drank at least five eight ounce glasses of water per day were 54% less likely to have a fatal heart attack then those who drank two or fewer. According to the researchers, the water dilutes the blood making it less likely to clot. Drink plenty of water, five to eight glasses per day minimum.

Keywords: Fat Loss, Weight Loss, Get Trim and Fit, Healthy Heart, Look Younger, Primary

---

Habit 23

Eat in a Well-Lit Room to Prevent Binge Eating

Benefits

Make it a habit to eat in a well-lit room. Did you know that binge eaters tend to eat in dark rooms? Recently a study was conducted by the University of California, Irvine. The study found that people who binged on snack foods tended to keep the lighting low while snacking.

The researchers suspected that this was a tactic that would allow the snackers to abandon the self-control that would typically keep them from overeating. The study author, Joseph Kasof, Ph.D., suggested that people who want to control their weight should turn up the lights on snacks instead of eating in near darkness. As he explains it, being in a situation that makes you feel like you are on stage can help you fight that urge to overeat.

Triggers

Place lamps close to where you usually eat snacks. Buy higher wattage bulbs and replace lower wattage bulbs.

Keywords: Fat Loss, Weight Loss, Get Trim and Fit, More Motivated

Habit 24

Weigh Yourself Once a Week

Make it a habit to weigh yourself once per week and record the results in your one-minute tracking log.

Benefits

You will have a detailed record of your weight losses and or gains. By referring to your one-minute tracking log, you will be able to quickly spot trends in your weight loss and make any necessary adjustments if you gain a couple of pounds. Researchers studied 3,000 people in a database called the National Weight Control Registry. These people had all lost over 30 pounds and had kept the weight off for more than a year. The study found that just about all of the participants weighed themselves on a regular basis.

Triggers

Pull your scale out of your closet and put it somewhere where you will see it more often.

Keywords: Fat Loss, Weight Loss, Get Trim And Fit, More Motivated

Habit 25

Carry a 32-Ounce Water Bottle Filled With Cold Water

Make it a habit to carry a 32-ounce water bottle with you during the day and drink from it periodically. Also remember to drink cold water whenever possible.

Benefits

Why is cold water beneficial? A gallon of cold water (40 degrees) requires 226 calories of energy. Cold water burns calories faster. By drinking cold water periodically during the day, you will burn more calories.

Habit Tips

Combine this habit with the brisk walking habit, carry cold water with you as you walk.

Triggers

Keep a 32-ounce water bottle near your front door so you will be reminded to fill it and bring it with you each time you leave the house.

Keywords: Fat Loss, Weight Loss, Get Trim and Fit

Healthy Heart Habits
and
Lower Cholesterol Habits

If you want to live to be 100 or older, you can't just sit around
waiting for it to happen. You have to get up each day and go after it!
– George Burns

◆

Habit 26

Start Your Day With Oatmeal For Energy, a Healthy Heart, and a Trim and Fit Body

Benefits

If you want lots of energy, a healthy heart, and a trim and fit body, you can't go wrong with making oatmeal in the morning a positive habit.

Healthy Heart

A study published June 3, 1999, by the *Journal of the American Medical Association* (JAMA), reinforced the fact that women can reduce their risk of heart disease by eating soluble fiber from cereals such as oatmeal. "The Nurses Health Study reported in JAMA is very important because it provides women with effective and practical information on how to reduce the risk for heart disease, which is the leading cause of death for women in this country," said Dr. Steve Ink, director of Nutrition Services, The Quaker Oats Company.

"The early results from these ongoing studies indicate that certain soluble fiber-containing grains – like oats – may work to lower risk for heart disease in several important ways." Daily consumption (five or more servings per week) of cold breakfast cereals reduced the risk for heart disease in women by 19 %, while oatmeal consumption reduced the risk for heart disease by 29 %," investigators at Pennsylvania State University, reported.

Long-Lasting Energy

Do you want to have sustained energy all day? Who doesn't? New research published in the *Journal of Applied Physiology* shows that oatmeal provides a slow-burning, sustained energy that lasts into the day. "Because oatmeal is rich in soluble fiber, its energy is released into the body slowly," said John Kirwan of the Noll Physiological Research Center at Pennsylvania State University, the study's author. "This gradual release helps conserve the body's energy stores during an active day, unlike a more rapidly-absorbed carbohydrate meal, which may leave you feeling tired soon after eating."

Another benefit that oatmeal provides in your quest for a trim and fit body and a healthy heart is that it is extremely filling. Start off your day with a bowl of oatmeal, and you will be less likely to snack before lunchtime.

Habit Tips

Here are some tips for making oatmeal even more nutritious and healthy for you:

- ❑ Stir in a small amount of good fats – almond or cashew butter.

- ❑ Try adding all-natural apple sauce for a sweeter flavor or add 100% fruit spread. (Berries have many health benefits.)

- ❑ Add a tablespoon of soy protein after cooking and get the combined benefits of soy and oats.

Keywords: More Energy, Fat Loss, Weight Loss, Get Trim and Fit, Healthy Heart, Lower Cholesterol, Primary

Habit 27

Eat Fish at Least Twice a Week

Benefits

If you want a healthy heart, make it a habit to eat fish at least twice a week. The American Heart Association recently released guidelines for the consumption of fish. According to their guidelines, you should eat two, three-ounce servings of a fatty fish like salmon, tuna, or mackerel every week to help lessen your risk of developing heart disease.

Why is fish so good for your heart? Fish contain omega 3 fatty acids which have been shown to stabilize blood sugar, decrease the risk of coronary artery disease, and increase mental function. Eating more fish can also help you lower your LDL (bad) cholesterol and raise HDL (good) cholesterol.

Triggers

Keep cans of tuna fish in your pantry, and frozen fish fillets in your freezer.

Keywords: Healthy Heart, Lower Cholesterol, Less Stress, Stabilize Insulin, Primary

Habit 28

Incorporate Workouts Into Your Daily Routine

Benefits

As you go about your daily routine, make it a habit to incorporate workout moves into your actions. You can turn any activity, such as gardening, washing your car, mowing the lawn, into a muscle building, calorie burning workout. Remember, your goal is to make these small habits a part of your lifestyle; they will become second nature to you and you will reap the benefits in the long term.

❑ Do leg lunges while mowing the lawn.
❑ Do lunges and squats while you are at the copier or fax machine. (Forget the funny looks from co-workers you are getting in shape and they will probably join you.)
❑ When you are washing your car, concentrate on doing quick circles with your arms in both directions.
❑ Do leg squats while lifting plants during gardening activities.

Habit Tips

Review your daily activities and look for actions that you can incorporate workouts into. Make a mental note to start your workout when you start the activity.

Keywords: Healthy Heart, Weight Loss, Fat Loss, Get Trim and Fit, More Energy, Increased Strength, Build Muscle, Stronger Bones, Better Sleep

Habit 29

Substitute Bad Fat Snacks With Healthy Good Fat Nuts

Benefits

If you make it a habit to eat "good fat" nuts like almonds, macadamia nuts, cashews and pecans instead of "bad fat" chips and crackers, you will reap a wealth of benefits. Nuts provide you with healthy omega fatty acids and monosaturated fats. Here are just a few of the benefits this positive habit will provide you:

❑ Recent studies have shown that people who eat nuts on a regular basis have less heart disease then people who stay away from them. In fact, one study found that you can lower your heart attack risk by as much as 50% by consuming nuts that are rich in omega-9s at least five times a week.

❑ New research from Texas A&M University shows that a heart-healthy diet containing pecans can help to control cholesterol levels and other biomarkers of heart disease risk just as effectively as the American Heart Association's (AHA) Step 1 diet.

Keywords: Fat Loss, Weight Loss, Healthy Heart, Get Trim and Fit, Lower Cholesterol

Habit 30

Floss Your Teeth Regularly for a Healthy Heart

Benefits

You might be saying, "Floss my teeth, what does that have to do with my heart?" Believe it or not, it has a lot to do with the health of your heart. Flossing is not only good oral hygiene, it can also help in reducing a more serious threat to your health.

The risk for heart disease among people with gum disease is double that of people who don't have gum disease. The risk for stroke is even higher; You are three times more likely to have a stroke, if you have gum disease. If you want to protect your heart, and brain, make this one of your positive habits.

Triggers

Keep a package of dental floss next to your night stand.

Keywords: Healthy Heart, Reduced Stroke Risk, Healthier Teeth

Habit 31

Substitute Whole-Grain Bread For White Bread

Benefits

Make it a habit to eat whole-grain bread instead of white bread. A 2002 *American Journal of Clinical Nutrition* study found that a diet rich in whole, unrefined grains which are an excellent source of fiber, may help to lower the risk of heart disease and type-2 diabetes.

Dietary fiber may also help lower your cholesterol as well as help to prevent certain types of cancer. Other studies have shown that people who have a lot of fiber in their diet, are happier. Whole-grain bread contains significantly more nutrients then bleached white bread. Do you know why we have white bread? White bread was created because of a need to increase the shelf life of bread products.

Triggers

Toss out your white bread and keep a loaf of whole grain bread in your pantry. Order whole-grain bread when you eat out.

Keywords: Healthy Heart, Lower Cholesterol, Lower Cancer Risk, Reduced Diabetes Risk, More Motivated, Less Stress

◆
_____

Habit 32

Paint Your Plate with Vibrant Colors for Vibrant Health

_____

Benefits

Make it a habit to eat meals that consist of many varieties of colors. Why? A diet rich in the most colorful fruits and vegetables gives you the beneficial compounds that you need to help prevent heart attack, cancer, stroke, and diabetes? The color pigments in the fruits and vegetables are potent antioxidants; the more colors you see, the better.

Blue, purple and red foods are antioxidants, and some are also anti-inflammatories. The National Cancer Institute has launched a campaign called "Savor the Spectrum." They are urging Americans to eat fruits and vegetables that consist of the primary color groups: red, yellow, orange, green, blue/purple, with garlic and white onions.

Loreli Disogra, R.D., Director of the National Cancer Institute program says, "When you see colors on your plate you know you are doing good things for yourself."

Triggers

Think of your dinner plate as an artist's canvas. Try to paint the most colorful picture you can, using food as your paint. When you shop, look for the brightest colors in the produce department.

Keywords: Lower Cancer Risk, Healthy Heart, Live Longer, Get Trim and Fit, Primary

_____

Habit 33

Take at Least 100 Units of Vitamin E per Day

Benefits

The primary use of Vitamin E is as an antioxidant. It helps to protect against strokes, cancer and heart disease. Studies have shown that low levels of Vitamin E are predictive of heart disease. A Harvard-based study determined that men who had consumed a minimum of 100 units of Vitamin E each day, had almost half the risk of coronary heart disease of the men in the study who had consumed less then 7 units of Vitamin E daily. If you want to reduce your risk of heart disease, cancer, and stroke make it a habit to take a minimum of 100 units of Vitamin E each day.

Triggers

Buy natural Vitamin E in minimum 100 unit doses, and put them on the top shelf of your refrigerator. Note: look for "d-Alpha tocopherol" on the label to make sure you are getting natural Vitamin E.

Keywords: Healthy Heart, Lower Cancer Risk, Reduced Stroke Risk

Habit 34

Benefits

Many studies have shown that your body will burn fat faster if you increase your water intake. Order a large pitcher of water every time you order dinner out, and drink more water during dinner. This is a healthy heart habit that will help you reduce body fat.

Triggers

The waiter or waitress approaching your table is your cue.

Keywords: Fat Loss, Weight Loss, Get Trim and Fit

Habit 35

Eat an Apple Every Day

Benefits

OK, you have probably heard this a million times, "an apple a day keeps the doctor away." It really is true, and here are the reasons you should make this a daily positive habit:

- ❑ A medium apple contains 5 grams of healthy heart fiber.
- ❑ Apples have virtually no fat.
- ❑ Flavonoids and other chemicals in apples can help to decrease your risk for getting colon and lung cancer.
- ❑ The tannins in apples help prevent tooth decay, gum disease, and urinary tract infections.
- ❑ The fiber, pectin and antioxidants in apples can help to raise HDL (good) cholesterol and lower LDL (bad) cholesterol.

Triggers

Keep a bowl of fresh apples on your kitchen counter or table.

Keywords: Healthy Heart, Lower Cholesterol, Lower Cancer Risk

Habit 36

Refer to Yourself Less in Conversations

Believe it or not, people who speak more about others then themselves in conversations are less likely to suffer from heart disease! Larry Scherwitz, Ph.D., a research scientist from the University of California, conducted an innovative study in which he taped the conversations of approximately 600 men; A third of these men were suffering from heart disease; the rest of the men were all healthy.

He counted how often they used the words *I, me,* and *mine* in conversations. When he compared his results, he discovered that the men who used those words the most had the highest risk for heart trouble. Yes, self-centeredness is indeed a risk factor for coronary heart disease

Triggers

Your triggers are the words *I, me,* and *mine.* Try to keep track of how often you use these words. Your goal is to use them less.

Keywords: Healthy Heart

Habit 37

When Stress Hits, Count to Ten

Benefits

Make it a habit to slowly count to ten the moment you encounter a stressful situation. This slow, ten-second countdown may be just enough to cool you down. Researchers at Johns Hopkins University say that men who respond to stress with anger are three times more likely to be diagnosed with heart disease and five times more likely to have a heart attack before the age of 55. As you count down, take a few deep breaths; this will also help calm your nerves and relieve stress.

Triggers

Consider stress as your cue to begin your countdown.

Keywords: Healthy Heart, Less Stress

Positive Supplementation Habits

The human body has one ability not possessed by any
machine–the ability to repair itself.
– George E. Crile, Jr., M.D.

I am always amazed at the response I usually get when I ask
people this question: "Do you supplement your diet with vitamins and
minerals?" The response I usually get is, " I don't need to, I eat a well-
balanced diet." What is so amazing to me about this response, is that it
reveals how little most people know about what they are actually getting
in their so-called balanced diet.

The human body is an extremely complicated machine; it requires a
wide variety of nutrients to maintain a constant state of health. But the
simple truth is that the average American does not get the nourishment
needed to maintain a health body free of disease. Why? The answer goes
back to the days of your grandparents, a time when local farms were the
main source of food, when bread was baked fresh every day with fresh-
harvested grains. Milk came from cows who lived in natural, stress-free
environments, and were not injected with hormones and antibiotics.

Yes, our grandparents ate food that was filled with the essential
nutrients that the human body requires to stay healthy. Today's food
is quite different from the food our grandparents ate; it is grown in
large farms where the mineral contents of the soil is depleted due to
over-farming. Did you know that an ounce of spinach grown on a local
farm in the 1940s contains five times more iron then an ounce of spinach

commercially grown today? It is almost impossible to get the essential nutrients needed to maintain a healthy body by simply consuming today's commercially processed foods. You can protect your health by making it a positive habit to supplement your diet with vitamins, minerals, and other nutritional supplements.

A report issued in September 2002 by the *Journal of the American Medical Association* has recognized the link between vitamins and the reduced risk of chronic diseases, like cancer, cardiovascular disease, and osteoporosis. The report states, "Most people do not consume an optimal amount of all vitamins by diet alone," the report recommends, "all adults should take one multivitamin daily. Recent evidence has shown that suboptimal levels of vitamins, even well above those causing deficiency syndromes, are risk factors for chronic diseases."

This is the reason why my answer is yes when many people ask me, "Is it necessary to supplement vitamins, minerals, and other nutrients?" It is virtually impossible to provide your body with all the essential nutrients without supplementing. This is why supplementation has become popular today; our current foods simply do not contain the nutrients we need to stay healthy.

It is not within the scope of this book to provide you with all of the information available today on nutritional supplements. There are many excellent books written on the subject listed in the resource section in the back of this book. I recommend that you educate yourself further on the many health benefits that nutritional supplements can bring to your life. You, and you alone are responsible for your health. It is your life; choose to learn more about the things you can do to improve you health. As you will see by the habits to follow, there are many supplements that can become positive habits. They can have a significant effect on your overall health and well being.

◆
Habit 38

Visualize and Affirm the Benefits of
Supplements as You Take Them

Benefits

This is a very powerful habit. Have you heard of the placebo effect? The placebo effect is an observable, measurable, improvement in one's health, not attributable to a specific treatment. A sugar pill is an example. Numerous scientific studies have shown that people can experience improvements in their health when they take a sugar pill that they have been told is actually a drug. They get better because they believe that they have just taken a powerful drug that will make them better. The placebo effect is an excellent example of the mind-body connection.

Why is the placebo effect so important? It shows how powerful the mind can be even when the substance taken is inert. Imagine how powerful a visualization can be when you take supplements that provide actual benefits. Each time you take a supplement, visualize and affirm that you are receiving its benefits now. Here are some examples:

❏ Scientific studies have shown people who have high levels of selenium in their blood have less risk of getting certain cancers. As you take your selenium supplement each day, imagine that your body is now cancer proof.

❑   As you take vitamin E supplements, imagine that
    your heart is getting stronger and healthier. You get the picture.

Do this with all your positive habits. Visualize that you are already
receiving their benefits.

*Keywords: Fat Loss, Weight Loss, Get Trim and Fit, Live Longer, Lower Cancer Risk,
Less Stress, More Motivated, Stronger Immune System, Primary*

Habit 39

Take a Multivitamin Every Day

Benefits

The *Journal of the American Medical Association* has now recognized that there is a link between vitamins and the reduced risk of chronic diseases, like cancer, cardiovascular disease and osteoporosis.

The report says "Most people do not consume an optimal amount of all vitamins by diet alone" the report further recommends "all adults should take one multivitamin daily." In fact it states, "Recent evidence has shown that suboptimal levels of vitamins, even well above those causing deficiency syndromes, are risk factors for chronic diseases." Consequently, "A large proportion of the general population is apparently at increased risk. We recommend multivitamins, rather than individual vitamins, because multivitamins are simpler to take, and because a large proportion of the population needs supplements of more than one vitamin." By making it a habit to take a multivitamin every day, you will be protecting the most valuable asset you have, your health.

Triggers

Keep a container of multivitamins next to your breakfast cereal.

Keywords: Healthy Heart, Lower Cancer Risk, Stronger Bones

Habit 40

Take CoQ10 for a Healthy Heart and Increased Energy

Benefits

CoQ10 is found in every cell of the body; it is a naturally occurring nutrient. CoQ10 is most commonly found in fish and meats. It is a powerful antioxidant, and plays a major role in the energy system of our cells; it helps cells produce more energy. For many years, medical researchers have noticed that patients with heart failure had lower levels of CoQ10. Supplementing with CoQ10 restored their levels and also resulted in clinical improvements. Here is what some of the experts are saying about CoQ10:

Energy is life, and CoQ10 is a crucial component of
the energy cycle and therefore of life itself.
– Emile Bliznakov, and Gerald Hunt, co-authors,
The Miracle Nutrient: Coenzyme Q10

It's (CoQ10) a heart medicine used around the world, and if your doctor doesn't know about it, you can easily get it on your own; it could save your life.
– Jean Carper, Author of the best-seller *Miracle Cures.*

Studies show that most people with congestive heart failure have a deficiency of CoQ10 in their heart muscle. The lower the levels, the worse the congestive heart failure. But studies also show that patients who were supposed to die 15 years ago from congestive heart failure are still alive today primarily because of taking Coenzyme Q10 daily.

– William Lee Cowden, MD, Cardiologist

If you want to have a healthy heart and improved energy levels, consider CoQ10. Most experts recommend taking no more then 60 mg. daily. Check with your physician or nutritionist.

Habit Tips

If you want to have sustained energy all day, try combining this habit with Habit 26 oatmeal for more energy.

Keywords: Healthy Heart, More Energy

Habit 41

Soy

Benefits

As discussed in previous habits, soy provides many health benefits. Soy is recommended as a primary supplementation habit. A study published in the May 2001 issue of *Cancer, Epidemiology, Bimarkers, and Prevention* showed that for each incremental increase in the intake of soy during adolescence, there was a reduction in the risk of breast cancer. Women who had the highest consumption of soy had only half the risk of women with the lowest intake. In addition, there have been studies that have shown a reduced risk of colon cancer and prostate cancer with the increased consumption of soy.

Additional benefits of soy:

❑ The latest research shows that a diet rich in soy is associated with improved breast, colon, and prostate health; reduced menstrual disturbances, and stronger bones.

❑ Soy helps you lose weight by reducing your fat intake, calories, and cholesterol while improving your energy levels.

❑ Soy helps reduce menopausal symptoms.

❑ Genistein is a chemical compound that is found in soy; it has been cited as an anticancer agent.
Dr. Lee, of the Norris Comprehensive Cancer Center at the University of Southern California School of Medicine says, "The much lower risk of breast, colon, and prostate cancers in Asians who consume 20 to 30 times more soy per capita than Americans has raised the question whether compounds in the soy diet may be acting as a natural chemopreventive agent."

Habit Tips

There are many ways to incorporate soy into your diet, and contrary to popular belief, soy can be an extremely tasty food. Here are some tips:

❑ Make a delicious soy protein shake with your favorite juice.
❑ Try the many varieties of soy burgers, hot dogs, cheeses.
❑ Check out the variety of soy recipes on the Internet; just go to a search engine like yahoo or lycos and type in "soy recipes."

Triggers

Keep containers of soy protein in your pantry. Purchase soy cheeses, soy hot dogs, tofu and other soy products.

Keywords: Fat Loss, Weight Loss, Healthy Heart, Get Trim and Fit, Live Longer, Lower Cancer Risk, Increased Strength, More Energy, Prostate Health, Stronger Bones, Primary

Habit 42

Apple Cider Vinegar Cocktail

You have heard the popular saying "an apple a day keeps the doctor away." Apples are nutritional powerhouses, and apple cider vinegar also packs a powerful nutritional punch. In 400 BC, Hippocrates, the father of medicine, treated his patients with natural apple cider vinegar for its powerful healing and cleansing qualities.

Paul C. Bragg, legendary health crusader, and author of many books on health including, the *Apple Cider Vinegar Miracle Health System* says, "Pure organic undistilled apple cider vinegar can really be called one of nature's most perfect foods." Raw, organic apple cider vinegar will provide your body with potassium, enzymes, and other vitamins needed to maintain a healthy digestive and circulatory system. Here are some of the benefits that apple cider vinegar provides:

- ❑ Helps to control and normalize body weight
- ❑ Helps improve digestion
- ❑ Helps remove toxins from your body
- ❑ Helps to relieve muscle stiffness
- ❑ Is a natural antibiotic
- ❑ Helps to keep skin, tissues and joints youthful
- ❑ Helps fight arthritis and removes crystals and toxins from joints, tissues and organs

Habit Tips

Make an apple cider vinegar cocktail with 1 tablespoon natural apple cider vinegar, and 1 tablespoon honey. Mix them together and add a small amount of pure water or apple juice. Drink this healthy cocktail every morning. Make sure you buy only pure, undistilled apple cider vinegar. You can find it at your local health food store.

Triggers

Keep a bottle of natural organic apple cider vinegar on your kitchen shelf.

Keywords: Weight Loss, Get Trim and Fit,

Habit 43

Take Selenium to Reduce Your Cancer Risk

Benefits

Selenium is an essential trace mineral; it is also a powerful antioxidant. Selenium helps to protect cells against the effects of free radicals. Numerous studies show that selenium can help reduce the risk of cancer:

❑ A study in Finland showed that men who had low levels of selenium in their bodies were more then three times more likely to develop lung cancer then men who had higher levels.

❑ Research in the United States has shown that the states that had the lowest levels of the mineral selenium in their soil had the highest levels of cancer.

❑ A study that was published in the *Journal of the American Medical Association* showed that selenium supplementation led to a 50% reduction in cancer mortality.

Keywords: Lower Cancer Risk, Live Longer

Habit 44

Garlic

Benefits

Most people think of garlic as a flavoring agent to spice up foods. Garlic is an extremely powerful functional food; it contains a number of organic compounds that help protect the human body. Here are a few of the benefits that garlic provides:

- ❏ Lowers blood pressure
- ❏ Lowers LDL (bad) cholesterol
- ❏ Has powerful antioxidant properties
- ❏ Helps regulate blood sugar
- ❏ Is a potent natural antibiotic

Make it a habit to add fresh garlic to your food and order foods prepared with garlic. If you suffer from high blood pressure, many doctors recommend consuming one clove of raw garlic per day.

Triggers

Many people have raw garlic displayed in their kitchen in baskets or bags hanging from the ceiling. This is a great visual cue to remind you to add it to your favorite dish.

Keywords: Healthy Heart, Lower Cholesterol, Lower Blood Pressure, Stabilize Insulin

Habit 45

Lecithin

Benefits

Lecithin is a fat like substance that is composed mostly of choline, linoleic acid, B vitamins, and inositol. It has been shown to provide a variety of positive benefits to health.

- ❏ Even though it is a fatty substance, its high amounts of choline help the body burn fat faster.

- ❏ It helps protect cells from oxidation.

- ❏ It provides support to the liver.

- ❏ It has been shown to help lower blood cholesterol.

- ❏ It helps to protect against heart attack and stroke.

Habit Tips

Lecithin is typically derived from soybeans, and is available at health food stores as a powder or in capsules. See Habit 3 for a great protein shake recipe using lecithin.

Keywords: Fat Loss, Weight Loss, Get Trim and Fit, Lower Cancer Risk, Healthy Heart

Habit 46

Probiotics

Benefits

An important factor in achieving optimum health is a healthy digestive tract. Probiotics contain friendly bacteria that help you to maintain a favorable balance of bacteria in your digestive tract.

Bob Roberts, a food scientist at Penn State's College of Agricultural Sciences, says, "Probiotics have been shown to enhance immune response and to decrease cholesterol." These helpful bacteria provide many health benefits.

- ❑ Better digestion and assimilation of food
- ❑ Production of lactic acid and important digestive enzymes
- ❑ Better digestion of lactose, a milk sugar which some people have trouble digesting
- ❑ Enhanced immune system
- ❑ Lower cholesterol

People who are taking antibiotics should supplement with probiotics since the antibiotics kill off the good bacteria along with the bad bacteria.

Keywords: Stronger Immune System, Lower Cholesterol, Get Trim and Fit

Habit 47

Grape Seed Extract

Benefits

The French consume a diet that is high in saturated fat and they also smoke in excess, yet they are known for having the lowest rate of heart disease of any of the Westernized countries. Researchers believe that their secret to good health can be found in the red wine that they drink. Grape seed flavonoids are known to be very powerful antioxidants.

Antioxidants can protect your health by providing electrons that neutralize free radicals. Free radicals are molecules that have unpaired electrons, they can have a negative affect on your immune system, this can lead to degenerative diseases including cancer and heart disease and can also cause premature aging.

Free radicals are produced as a result of exposure to environmental pollutants, drugs, alcohol, sunlight, radiation, cigarette smoke and from the normal oxygen metabolism that occurs in your body. If you want to look younger and live longer, it is important to reduce the amount of free radicals in your body. Antioxidants help you do that.

You are probably aware of other popular antioxidants such as vitamins E and C, selenium, beta carotene, and bioflavonoids. Grape seed extract as an antioxidant is 50 times more powerful then vitamin E and 20 times more powerful then vitamin C. Here are some of the benefits that grape seed extract provides:

- ☐ Helps in reducing aging of the skin.
- ☐ Helps to increase capillary strength and also helps to enhance vascular function.
- ☐ Helps strengthen the heart.
- ☐ Helps stimulate the growth of healthy hair.
- ☐ Provides a synergistic effect with vitamin E and C.
- ☐ Helps to reduce LDL (bad) cholesterol.

Habit Tips

Take this supplement with fresh orange juice and vitamin E, for a powerful free radical fighting cocktail.

Keywords: Look Younger, Live Longer, Lower Cancer Risk, Healthy Heart

Habit 48

Brush Your Skin With a Dry Skin Brush Before Showering

Benefits

This habit is not a supplementation habit, however it is a health and fitness habit. Your skin is the largest organ in your body. It is also one of the most important organs for the elimination of toxins. Dry skin brushing helps rid your body of toxins. Here are some additional benefits that dry skin brushing provides:

- ❏ It helps to remove cellulite
- ❏ It removes dead layers of skin
- ❏ It helps to strengthen your immune system
- ❏ Stimulates your lymph glands which helps your body to perform better
- ❏ Increases renewal of your cells
- ❏ It helps improve blood circulation
- ❏ It makes your skin look younger

Buy a natural-skin brush at your local health food store or natural market. A natural-bristle brush will not scratch your skin. Make sure you get a brush with a long handle so you can reach your back.

Brush your body before a bath or shower. Brush your skin when it is dry, and brush in the direction of your heart. Do counterclockwise circular strokes. Start out with your feet, then brush your entire body with the exception of your face and your nipples. When you are finished, take a warm shower or bath and follow that with a cool rinse. You will feel invigorated, and your skin will rejuvenate with each brushing.

Triggers

Place your dry skin brush someplace close to your bath or shower, where it will be visible.

Keywords: Better Skin, Look Younger, Stronger Immune System

Positive Sleeping Habits

By learning to sleep well, you will also feel more
energy and joy and be more productive, feel calmer and more optimistic.
– Gregg D. Jacobs Ph.D., author of *Say Good night to Insomnia*

Habit 49

Don't Toss and Turn in Bed

Don't toss and turn in bed. If you have trouble falling asleep for 20 minutes or more, leave your bedroom. Go to another room in your house until your are tired. Then return to your bed.

Benefits

Your bed becomes a very powerful cue for sleep. If you toss and turn, your mind will associate your inability to fall asleep with your bed. Instead, leave your bedroom and go to another room to conduct another activity, such as reading or watching television.

When you start to feel sleepy, return to your bed. By doing this your mind will see your bed as a place where you fall asleep, and it will become easier to fall asleep regularly.

Keywords: Better Sleep, More Energy, More Motivated, Less Stress, Stronger Immune System

Habit 50

Engage in Relaxing Activities One Hour Before Bedtime

Benefits

There are many activities you can engage in that will relax your mind and make it easier to fall asleep. Read a book or listen to relaxing music. Many experts suggest going for a walk 2 to 3 hours before bedtime. Walking is a calming activity that will help prepare your body for sleep.

Keywords: Better Sleep, More Energy, More Motivated, Less Stress, Stronger Immune System

Habit 51

Exercise Three to Six Hours Before Bedtime

Benefits

When we sleep our body temperatures drop. Exercise causes your body temperature to fall 3 to 6 hours after the exercise. If you have trouble sleeping, make it a habit to work out 3 to 6 hours before your bedtime. Your body temperature will drop faster and that will help you fall asleep faster.

Triggers

Set an alarm clock to go off 3 to 6 hours before your bedtime. This will be your cue to begin exercising.

Keywords: Better Sleep, More Energy, More Motivated, Less Stress, Stronger Immune System

Habit 52

Change Your Sleep Self-Talk

Did your know that the way you talk to yourself about sleep during the day affects your sleep at night? Many people fall into this negative self-talk trap. If they have a bad night's sleep, they will say things like:

"I did not get enough sleep last night; I am going to feel terrible today."

"I never sleep well anymore."

"I just know I am going to have trouble sleeping tonight."

The way you think during the day can affect how you sleep. Consciously changing those thoughts is called cognitive restructuring. Gregg Jacobs Ph.D.., author of *Say Good Night to Insomnia,* says, "In short, cognitive re-structuring will be the initial catalyst for improving your sleep and yourself in a number of important ways." Make it a habit to replace your negative self-talk about sleep with positive self-talk:

" I know I will sleep well tonight."

"My day is not determined by just the amount of sleep I got last night."

"Every day, my sleep is improving."

Benefits

There are many benefits to cognitive restructuring:

❑ You will learn how to better control your negative thoughts and emotions.

❑ You will feel more in control over your sleep.

❑ You will feel less frustrated, and frustration can cause insomnia.

Triggers

Your negative daily thoughts are your triggers. When you find that you are having a negative thought about sleep, replace it immediately with a positive thought.

Keywords: Better Sleep, More Energy, More Motivated, Less Stress, Stronger Immune System

Words are clothes that thoughts wear.
— Samuel Butler

CHAPTER 4

Positive Habits for Success and Relationships

You can have everything in life you want,
if you will just help enough other people get what they want.
– Zig Ziglar

Positive Success Habits

Always bear in mind that your own resolution to success
is more important then any other one thing.
— Abraham Lincoln

What can positive success habits do for you? Everyone wants to be successful, but not many people are. Positive habits can help you achieve success automatically. Here are just a few of the benefits you will achieve by acquiring the habits in this chapter:

❑ Your mental attitude will be more positive automatically.
❑ You will have better control of your emotions.
❑ You will have better self-esteem.
❑ You will be more confident and optimistic.
❑ You will set and achieve goals automatically.
❑ You will have an improved mental picture of your life.
❑ You will become more success oriented.
❑ Your positive success habits will help you to eliminate negative thinking.
❑ You will be happier with yourself and others.

◆
_____

Habit 53

Make It a Habit to Set Goals

_____

Benefits

It is almost impossible to overestimate the value of goal-setting as a positive habit. It is recommended as a primary habit because it can truly be life changing.

Research studies have shown that people who regularly set goals are far more likely to be successful then people who do not. Napoleon Hill, author of the best-seller, *Think and Grow Rich,* once said, "Definiteness of purpose is the starting point of all achievement, and its lack is the stumbling block for ninety eight out of every one hundred people because they never really define their goals and start toward them."

A study was done to determine the importance of goal setting. College students who had gone on to achieve great success in business were asked to list their habits. The students who had made a habit of setting goals were in the top 3% of earnings in the population!

Goal setting is simple, yet 97% of the population never do it. By making goal setting a habit, you can start placing yourself in the top 3% of the population of successful people. Your goal-setting habit can help you reach any of your goals, regardless of whether they are for business, personal, relationships, and so on.

Here are some simple steps to help you start your goal-setting habit:

Step 1 Define your destinations, write them down, and be very specific; capture your goals on paper.

Step 2 Determine what the time line is for reaching your goals; set specific deadlines for each goal.

Step 3 Identify any obstacles that may stand in your way, list them, and state how you plan to overcome them.

Step 4 Make a list of the people and/or organizations who will help you reach your goals.

Habit Tips

You can combine this habit with virtually any of your other habits. As an example, if weight loss is one of your destinations, make it a habit to set specific goals for the amount of weight you want to lose and a time line for reaching that goal. If a healthy heart is your destination, you can set goals for exercising and lowering your cholesterol.

Triggers

Keep a note pad with you at all times listing your goals, time lines, and plans to reach your goals.

Keywords: Success, More Motivated, Less Stress, Improved Self-Esteem, Primary

Habit 54

Make It a Habit to Break Large Jobs Into Small Pieces

Large jobs are always easier when you break them down into smaller pieces. As an example, when I first sat down to write this book, it seemed to be such a huge project that it quickly overwhelmed me. By breaking it down into many pieces (chapters in this case) and by working on each chapter as a separate small piece, it became much more manageable and less daunting. The most important thing is to just start somewhere and keep moving.

Benefits

This habit will make all of your big projects seem smaller and easier to manage.

Keywords: Success, More Motivated, Less Stress

Habit 55

Make It a Habit to View Your Failures as Stepping Stones to Your Success

A failure should not be viewed as the end of the story but instead as a stepping-stone to a larger success.
Charles C. Manz, author of *The Power Of Failure*

Benefits

Every time you fail at something, make it a habit to stop and visualize the failure as a necessary step to success. Thomas Edison had failure after failure in his attempts to invent a working light bulb. In fact, it took over 1100 experiments before he succeeded! Each one of those failed experiments was a necessary step to his eventual success in the greatest of all of his inventions.

Triggers

Failure is your cue to stop and think about failure as a stepping stone to success.

Keywords: Success, More Motivated

Habit 56

Be More Productive With the 4-D Habit

Benefits

There is a very simple formula to help you prevent work overload. Every time you are faced with a new task to perform, apply the 4 D's as listed below. You will find that your workload will be reduced as you apply this screening and decision making tool to each task. Decide on the most appropriate choice – and take action.

- ❑ Do It Now – take immediate action, do the task right away, don't procrastinate.
- ❑ Dump It Now – make a quick decision and dump the task.
- ❑ Delegate It – give the task to someone else. This is a very critical aspect of time management. Your time is valuable; make it a habit to work on tasks that you do best and delegate the tasks that can be performed by someone else.
- ❑ Defer the Task – make an immediate decision to postpone the task to a later time. Make sure to schedule a time to complete it.

Triggers

Your triggers for this habit are the actions associated with receiving a new task such as by mail, a phone call, an E-mail, and so on.

Keywords: Success, Less Stress

Habit 57

Read Ten Pages of a Book Each Night

Benefits

The average book is approximately 220 pages long. If you make this a positive habit, you will have read one book every 22 days! You can increase your knowledge substantially in any subject matter you choose, either fiction or nonfiction. Even if your reading speed is average, you should be able to read 10 pages in 15 minutes or less. Imagine how much more knowledge you could gain if you read more then one book every month! As an added bonus, your sleep may improve.

Triggers

Keep books on your night stand.

Keywords: Success, Increased Intelligence, Better Sleep, Primary

Habit 58

List the Opportunities That Exist in Each One of Your Failures

Circumstances, what are circumstances?
I make circumstances.
– Napoleon

Benefits

Within every failure there lies an opportunity for you to turn some element of the it into a success. Look at your failures as an indication that you are breaking new ground. Carole Hyatt. author of *When Smart People Fail: Rebuilding Yourself For Success,* says, "If you haven't failed at least three times today, you haven't tried anything new." Review the steps you took leading up to the failure, very often you will see hidden opportunities.

Keywords: Success, More Motivated

♦

Habit 59

Listen to Audiotapes on Your Daily
Commute Instead of the Radio

Benefits

Commuting is probably the biggest waste of productive time in the civilized world. Think of the millions of hours every day that people simply sit behind the wheel and steer their cars while stuck in traffic. You can turn this into productive time that will allow you to increase your education significantly: increase your vocabulary, learn a foreign language, gain knowledge of virtually any subject under the sun. You can do all this while driving to and from work.

Triggers

Keep motivational and educational audiotapes on the front seat passenger side of your car.

Keywords: Success, More Motivated, Increased Intelligence, Positive Attitude, Improved Self-Esteem, Primary

Habit 60

Remember Names With This Association Habit

Benefits

If you are like many people, you forget the name of a person seconds after you have been introduced. Improved-memory experts will tell you that the best way to remember a person's name is to associate something about his or her visual appearance with the name. As an example, suppose you were just introduced to a man named Bill Smith. You notice that his face reminds you a little of former President Bill Clinton. Make a mental association of the name Bill Smith with the visual picture of the former president. The next time you see this person, you will be more likely to remember his name. If you are a business person, it is very important that you remember names. This habit will help you do just that.

Triggers

Your trigger for this habits is the action of shaking someone's hand or the words associated with an introduction, such as "Let me introduce you to Mr. Smith."

Keywords: Success

◆

Habit 61

Read Your Goals Aloud Every Day

If you do what you've always done,
you'll get what you've always gotten.
– Anthony Robbins

Benefits

By reading your goals aloud every day, you are reenforcing in your mind exactly what it is that you intend to achieve. By visualizing your goals every day, they become entrenched in your subconscious mind and you will gravitate towards the completion of those goals.

Triggers

Carry a note pad listing your goals with you at all times.

Keywords: Success, More Motivated, Less Stress, Improved Self-Esteem, Positive Attitude, Primary

Habit 62

Make It a Habit to Watch One Hour Less Television Each Day

Make it a habit to watch one hour less television each day. If you watch 5 hours now, make it 4. Replace that time with something more beneficial to your life, such as reading, relaxing, meditating, exercise, yoga.

Benefits

By reducing your television watching by one hour per day, you will free up 364 hours in one year; that's over 45 days of extra time you will have to spend on beneficial activities.

Triggers

Some televisions have built-in timers. Set your timer so that your television will shut off automatically one hour earlier than usual.

Keywords: Success, Less Stress, Increased Intelligence

Positive Habits for a Positive Attitude, More Motivation and Improved Self-Esteem

All successful people, men and women are big dreamers. They imagine what their future could be, ideal in every respect, and then they work every day toward their distant vision, that goal or purpose.

– Brian Tracy

Your attitude is the way that you feel about yourself, other people, a situation or a circumstance. Napoleon Hill, the author of the best-selling book, *Think and Grow Rich,* put it so eloquently when he said, "The only thing over which you have complete right of control at all times is your mental attitude. Right of control means that you can control it, it does not mean that you do control it, you must learn to exercise this right as a matter of habit." Think about the power of that statement and how it holds the key to building your positive attitude habits.

You have the right of control over your mental attitude. The purpose of the power of positive habits is to give you the information you need to exercise that right of control by the selective acquisition of positive habits. By doing this, you are creating a new mind set, a mind set geared towards success.

Step 1 is simple; you exercise the only thing for which you have complete and absolute control and that is your mental attitude. Remember, the knowledge contained in your new positive habits is backed by the work of some of the most brilliant minds of our time, and by many years of research.

Habit 63

Positive-Attitude Trigger Phrases

Benefits

Choose or create a positive mental attitude trigger phrase and repeat it aloud many times each day. As discussed earlier, a habit trigger is an event, action, or thought that helps to reenforce your positive habits. Your trigger phrases will help you to maintain a positive mental attitude. Choose or make up a positive phrase, such as

- ❑ "I know I can do it."
- ❑ "I can overcome any obstacle."
- ❑ "I am reaching my success goals every day."
- ❑ "I am getting stronger and stronger every day."
- ❑ "Every day I am getting closer and closer to my goals in life."
- ❑ "If I believe it I can achieve it."
- ❑ "Every day, my mental attitude is becoming more positive."
- ❑ "I am losing weight every day."
- ❑ "I am getting closer daily to my goal of a trim and fit body."

Habit Tips

Write down your trigger phrase on Post-it notes; place them on the mirror of your car, on your bathroom mirror, carry the note in your pocket. Repeat the phrase many times every day, remember to say it with emotion, believe it with all your heart. Make it a habit to repeat this phrase at least 30 times a day. Start your day with it.

The more you repeat your trigger phrases, the greater their effect will be on your attitude. Whenever a negative thought enters your mind, replace it with your positive-attitude trigger phrase. You will now be building success-oriented positive thought patterns. This habit will help you achieve a positive mental attitude automatically. Remember, your attitude is everything!

Triggers

Place Post-it notes in places where you will see them often.

Keywords: Success, More Motivated, Get Trim and Fit, Weight Loss, Fat Loss, Improved Self-Esteem, Positive Attitude, Less Stress, Primary

Habit 64

Make It a Habit to Engage in Random Acts of Kindness

Benefits

If you want an instant prescription for feeling better, then make it a habit to help another person for no reason at all. Here are some examples to get you started:

- ❏ Open a door for someone.
- ❏ Let someone get ahead of you in line.
- ❏ Help an elderly person cross the street.
- ❏ Put money in another person's parking meter.

Your benefits will be many; try it and see!

Keywords: Positive Attitude, Success, Less Stress, More Motivated

Habit 65

Eat More Fiber, Be Happier and Less Depressed

Benefits

Making it a habit to eat more fiber can actually make you a happier person. Researchers at Cardiff University in Wales who studied people that ate a lot of fiber found that they had fewer memory problems, enjoyed better moods, and they were less depressed. "The physical benefits of a high-fiber diet have been widely acknowledged amongst health care professionals for many years; however, this is the first time high-fiber intake has been associated with improved mental health," says researcher Andrew Smith, Ph.D.

Here are some tips to increase your daily intake of fiber:

❑ Eat five servings per day of fruits and vegetables.
❑ Eat bran cereals for breakfast.
❑ Eat brown rice instead of white rice.
❑ Replace white bread with whole grain bread.

Triggers

Keep more fruits and vegetables in your kitchen. Combine this with habit 26, oatmeal for energy.

Keywords: Success, More Motivated, Get Trim and Fit, Improved Self-Esteem, Positive Attitude, Healthy Heart, Lower Cholesterol

Habit 66

Motivate Yourself With Daily Music Triggers

Make a list of the songs that you love the most; songs that make you feel happy, joyous, excited, full of energy, and young at heart. Make a tape or CD of these songs. Play these songs at a designated time, such as on your way to or from work, or just when you want to be motivated.

Benefits

As you listen to these songs, your mood will be elevated. Picture yourself as succeeding in what is most important to you right now. Do this over and over again. You will find that music triggers will automatically motivate you and give you a feeling of power and well-being. I have been able to place myself in a better mood on cue by playing songs that make me feel good. You can learn more about motivation in Steve Chandler's excellent book, *100 Ways to Motivate Yourself.*

Triggers

Keep custom music tapes on the front seat of your car.

Keywords: Success, More Motivated, Improved Self-Esteem, Positive Attitude, Less Stress

Habit 67

Overcome Sorrow and Disappointment With Work

When you are disappointed, frustrated, and full of sorrow, make a plan to work at something and begin the work immediately. The action of the work will bring you back into a positive focus and help you to regain your positive attitude.

Benefits

As you progress through your work, your frustrations and disappointments will seem to melt away. Make this a positive habit, and you will benefit greatly.

Triggers

Feelings of disappointment, sorrow and frustration are your cues to begin working on something.

Keywords: Success, More Motivated, Improved Self-Esteem, Positive Attitude

Habit 68

Allow Ample Time When Driving to Appointments

Benefits

This may sound like a no-brainer, but think about the stress you incur when you rush to arrive to an appointment. This is a very common bad habit. Make it a habit to leave early, and schedule plenty of time to make it to your destination. Here are some of the important benefits this habit will provide to you:

❑ You will have less stress in your life, because being late causes more stress.

❑ People will think of you as a dependable person.

❑ You will be safer; people that rush to avoid being late are at a greater risk of getting into an accident.

❑ You will be calmer and have better control of your words and actions when you reach your appointment.

Keywords: Success, Less Stress, Healthy Heart

Habit 69

Make It a Habit to Reflect More and Risk More

Benefits

Sociologist Dr. Anthony Campolo conducted a study in which 50 people over the age of 90 were asked to reflect upon their lives. Each study participant was asked a simple question: "If you had it to do over again, what would you do differently?" There were many answers, but there were two that dominated the study.

"I would reflect more," and "I would risk more."

Have you ever felt like you are too busy doing things and you are not spending enough time thinking about the things you are doing and why you do them? Have you ever thought about the opportunities you may have lost because you were afraid of taking risks? Perhaps these elders have a lesson for all of us. Reflect more, and take more risks.

Keywords: Positive Attitude, More Motivated, Less Stress

Habit 70

Get Smarter With Exercise Habits and Endorphins

Benefits

Do you need to be a little smarter today? Perhaps you have a test at school or an important job interview. Make it a habit to work out beforehand. A recent study suggests that endorphins, a hormone, may help to improve your intelligence, and exercise increases the amount of endorphins in your brain.

A study group took tests before and after running for 30 minutes. The researchers compared the study participant's brain waves during the two tests. The results were better scores, and faster brain activity on the tests that were taken after the run.

Keywords: Success, More Motivated, Improved Self-Esteem, Positive Attitude, Less Stress, Healthy Heart, Get Trim and Fit, Increased Intelligence

Habit 71

Boost Your Immune System With Laughter

Benefits

Make it a habit to watch funny videos when you feel under the weather, angry, or depressed. Last year, researchers at Loma Linda University published a study on the results of laughter on the immune system. They asked volunteers to watch a video of the comedian Gallagher smashing produce with a sledge hammer.

The researchers noticed that the volunteers showed significant improvements in several immune-system functions, such as natural killer cell activity. In another study, the same researchers found that merely anticipating watching a funny video improved moods such as anger, tension, and depression up to 2 days before actually watching the video. It really is true when they say "laughter is the best medicine."

Triggers

The next time you go to the video store, check out the comedy section. Look through your TV guide for funny shows, and set your VCR to record them. Feelings of depression or an illness coming on should be your trigger to watch something funny.

Keywords: Success, More Motivated, Improved Self-Esteem, Positive Attitude, Less Stress, Healthy Heart, Live Longer, Stronger Immune System

Positive Habits for Improved Relationships

I consider my ability to arouse enthusiasm among my people the greatest asset I possess, and the way to develop the best that is in a person is by appreciation and encouragement.

– Charles Schwab

♦
_____

Habit 72

Benefits

This and the next three habits are geared primarily toward men. If you really want to make your loved one happy, leave her notes of appreciation and love on a regular basis. Buy some Post-it notes and leave them where she is most likely to see them: in her car, on the bathroom window, and so on. Tell her how much you love her, give her kind words of encouragement and appreciation.

Triggers

Buy a package of Post-it notes and keep them somewhere handy.

Keywords: Improved Relationships With Wife or Loved One, Less Stress, Improved Self-Esteem, Improved Relationships, Primary

Habit 73

Brag About Your Wife to Others

Benefits

Make it a habit to brag about your wife in public. Whenever you are in a social setting, boast about the wonderful job she is doing as a mother, her new hair cut, the great promotion she just got at work, or anything else that you appreciate and are thankful for.

This is what Barbara DeAngelis, Ph.D., says about bragging about your wife in her book, *What Women Want Men to Know*: "When a women feels you are proud of her, she melts. You get many, many points for this. A compliment in public is worth ten in private."

Triggers

Your trigger for this habit is attending any social situation with your wife.

Keywords: Improved Relationships With Wife or Loved One

Habit 74

Make It a Habit to Listen to Your Wife

Benefits

This may sound like common sense, but apparently this is one of the biggest relationship problems between husbands and wives. In his best-selling book, *Men Are From Mars Women Are From Venus*, author John Gray, Ph.D., says, "The most frequently expressed complaint women have about men is that men don't listen."

If you make it a habit to spend more time listening to your wife, you will be addressing one of the biggest complaints wives have about their husbands. Your relationship will improve when your wife realizes that your responses are changing. You can extend this habit to the women you work with as well.

Triggers

The start of a conversation with your wife is your trigger for this important habit.

Keywords: Success, Improved Relationships With Wife or Loved One

Habit 75

Give Your Loved One Greeting Cards
on a Regular Basis

Benefits

Here is another good habit for men to acquire. Most men hate the idea of giving cards, but author Barbara De Angelis, Ph.D., an expert on relationships says "Think of cards as foreplay." She also says, "Every survey response I received contained a reference to cards."

It is apparent that women love cards, so make it a habit to give them regularly. Get creative: you can give her romantic cards, funny cards, you can even make up a card. Your benefits from this habit will be quite obvious. Try it and see.

Triggers

Buy an assortment of greeting cards and keep them in the glove compartment of your car or a desk drawer at work.

Keywords: Success, Improved Relationships With Wife or Loved One, Improved Relationships

Habit 76

Try to Understand the Other Person's Point of View

Benefits

Seems pretty simple, right? Henry Ford once said, "If there is one secret of success, it lies in the ability to get the other person's point of view, and see things from that person's angle, as well as from your own." Everyone wants something. Dale Carnegie once said, "Every act you have ever performed since the day you were born was performed because you wanted something." Even when you donate money to charity, you are doing so because you wanted to help someone. By knowing the other person's point of view, you will most likely also know what it is that they want the most.

Triggers

The beginning of any conversation should be a trigger for you to begin determining what the other person's point of view is.

Keywords: Success, Improved Relationships

◆

Habit 77

Show Your Sincere Appreciation to Others

When a study was done many years ago on wives who ran away from their husbands, it was determined that the number one reason they left their husbands was lack of appreciation. The great philosopher John Dewey once said that the greatest desire in human nature is the "desire to be important." When you show your appreciation to someone, you make them feel important.

Benefits

Your benefits will be many; and in fact, as strange as it seems, you will benefit more than the person who receives your appreciation. Everyone craves sincere, honest appreciation. Make this a permanent habit, and your life will be richly rewarded in ways that you cannot even imagine.

Keywords: Improved Relationships, Success, Improved Self Esteem, Primary

Habit 78

Make It a Habit to Force a Smile When You Are Angry

Benefits

Smiling is very calming and helps reduce stress. While this may sound silly, remember that stress is a major risk factor in heart disease. Whenever you feel angry, take a couple of deep breaths. Relax your shoulders and smile. As an added benefit, it is also very difficult to maintain an argument when one of the persons is smiling.

Triggers

Anger is your trigger, and it should be very easy to remember it, as it is not a subtle emotion.

Keywords: Success, Healthy Heart, Improved Relationships

Habit 79

Flirt With Your Husband or Boyfriend

Benefits

This habit and the next two are targeted for women. If you want to rekindle the romance in your relationship, make flirting a positive habit. Flirting is basically the expressing of admiration, flattery, desire and appreciation. Try to be alluring and suggestive. Think back to the days when you were courting and try to do the little things you used to do.

Habit Tips

❑ Make meaningful eye contact.

❑ Lean towards him and ask seductive questions in a whisper.

❑ Touch him and use suggestive body language.

❑ Uncross your legs and arms.

Keywords: Improved Relationships with Husband or Loved One

Habit 80

Turn Dinners Into Romantic Occasions

Benefits

It is often said that sex is the ultimate reinforcement for a man. If you want to keep your husband or boyfriend excited about your relationship, make it a habit to schedule at least one romantic dinner a month. Plan the evening and make the dinner special from start to finish, from arousal through to resolution. Include foods that have a high aphrodisiac quality, such as oysters, strawberries, and of course, chocolate. Create a romantic ambiance with candles and soft music. Champagne or wine can also be a part of the meal.

Triggers

Select a day each month for this romantic evening. Mark it on your calendar, the third Friday of every month, you get the idea.

Keywords: Improved Relationship with Husband or Loved One, Less Stress

Habit 81

Simple Moves to Make Your Man Happy

The best way to help a man grow, is to let go of
trying to change him in any way.
– John Gray, Ph.D.,
author of the *Men Are From Mars, Women Are From Venus Series*

Benefits

Sometimes it's the little things that make men the happiest. Write this short list of action items on a Post-it note and put it somewhere where only you will see it, like in your purse.

- ❑ Send him a love note in an envelope sealed with a kiss using your lipstick.
- ❑ Stop nagging him even if you know you are right.
- ❑ Don't make him choose between you and his football, basketball, golf, or fishing.
- ❑ If he gets lost while driving, tell him you loved the scenery, and you would not have seen it if he had taken the right route.
- ❑ If he makes a mistake, don't say "I told you so."

Keywords: Improved Relationship with Husband or Loved One

The Positive Habits Index

Use this index to locate habits by their keyword areas.

Resource Guide

The following is a list of suggested books and audiotapes that will help you reach your life destinations.

Suggested Reading

Success

10 Secrets for Success and Inner Peace
Wayne W. Dyer
Hay House; May 2002

100 Ways to Motivate Yourself
Steve Chandler
Career Press March 2001

Awaken the Giant Within: How to Take Immediate Control of Your Mental, Emotional, Physical & Financial Destiny!
Anthony Robbins, Frederick L. CoVan
Fireside; Reprint edition January 1993

Create Your Own Future: How to Master the 12 Critical Factors of Unlimited Success
Brian Tracy
John Wiley & Sons; August 2002

Don't Worry, Make Money
Richard Carlson
Hyperion, 1997

Giant Steps : Small Changes to Make a Big Difference : Daily
Lessons in Self-Mastery
Anthony Robbins
Fireside; September, 1994

How to Make Millions With Your Ideas: An Entrepreneur's Guide
Dan S. Kennedy
Plume; January, 1996

How to Reach Your Life Goals
Peter J. Daniels
Tabor House Publishing, 1985

Maximum Achievement: Strategies and Skills That Will Unlock
Your Hidden Powers to Succeed
Brian Tracy
Fireside. May, 1995

Positive Imaging
Norman Vincent Peale
Ballantine Books Reissue edition, September, 1996

Putting Your Faith Into Action Today!
Dr. Robert Schuller
Cathedral Ministries, 1998

Reinventing Yourself: How to Become the Person You've Always
Wanted to Be
Steve Chandler
Career Press; September, 1998

See You at the Top: 25th Anniversary Edition
Zig Ziglar
Pelican Pub Co; August, 2000

Success Bound: Breaking Free of Mediocrity
Randy Gilbert
Bargain Publishers Co., Inc., September, 2001

Success Through A Positive Mental Attitude
Napoleon Hill, W. Clement Stone
Prentice Hall

Success System That Never Fails
W. Clement Stone
Simon & Schuster, 1991

The 7 Habits Of Highly Effective People
Steven R. Covey
Simon and Schuster

The Alladin Factor
Jack Canfield and Mark Victor Hansen
Berkeley Books, Division of Oenuin Putnam, 1995

The Bible

The Greatest Secret In The World
Og Mandino
Bantam Books, 1972

The Millionaire Next Door
Thomas J. Stanley, William D. Danko
Longstreet Press, 1996

The Power Of Failure
Charles C. Manz
Berrett-Koehler Pub; May, 2002

The Power Of Focus
Jack Canfield, Les Hewitt, Mark Victor Hansen
Health Communications

The Power of Positive Thinking
Norman Vincent Peale
Ballantine Books Reissue edition, August, 1996

The Seven Spiritual Laws of Success: A Practical Guide to the
Fulfillment of Your Dreams
Deepak Chopra
Amber-Allen Pub; January, 1995

Think and Grow Rich
Napoleon Hill
Fawcett Crest Books/CBS, Inc
Division of Ballantine Books

When Smart People Fail: Rebuilding Yourself For Success
Carole Hyatt, Linda Gottlieb
Penguin USA May, 1993

Unlimited Power
Anthony Robbins
Simon and Schuster

Health & Fitness

8 Minutes In The Morning
Jorge Cruise, Anthony Robbins
Rodale Press; October, 2001

8 Weeks to Optimum Health
Andrew Weil M.D.,
Fawcett Books; Reissue edition July, 1998

Apple Cider Vinegar - Miracle Health System
Patricia Bragg, Paul C. Bragg
Health Science; January, 1999

Ageless Body, Timeless Mind: The Quantum Alternative to
Growing Old
Deepak, M.D. Chopra
Three Rivers Press; September 1998

Encyclopedia of Foods A Guide To Healthy Nutrition
Dole, David H. Murdock
Academic Press; December, 2001

Earl Mindell's Vitamin Bible for the 21st Century
Earl Mindell
Warner Books; May, 1999

Eating Well For Optimum Health: The Essential Guide to
Bringing Health and Pleasure Back to Eating
Andrew Weil
Quill; March, 2001

Fit for Life II: Living Health
Harvey Diamond , Marilyn Diamond
Warner Books; July 1993

Flax Your Way to Better Health
Jane Reinhardt-Martin
TSA Press; October, 2001

Get with the Program!
Bob Greene
Simon & Schuster; January 2002

Grow Younger, Live Longer: 10 Steps to Reverse Aging
David, Md Simon, Deepak, Md Chopra
Harmony Books; August, 2001

Healthy Heart: Keep Your Cardoiovascular System Healthy and Fit
at Any Age
Patricia Bragg, Paul C. Bragg
Health Science; February, 2001

Perfect Health: The Complete Mind Body Guide
Deepak, M.D. Chopra
Three Rivers Press; February, 2001

Perfect Weight: The Complete Mind/Body Program for Achieving
and Maintaining Your Ideal Weight (Perfect Health Library)
Deepak Chopra
Crown Pub; April, 1996

Quantum Healing: Exploring the Frontiers of Mind Body Medicine
Deepak Chopra
Bantam Books; May, 1990

Say Goodnight to Insomnia
Gregg D. Jacobs, Herbert Benson
Owl Books; November, 1999

Suzanne Somers' Eat, Cheat, and Melt the Fat Away
Suzanne Somers
Crown Pub; April, 2001

The 8-Week Cholesterol Cure: How to Lower Your Blood
Cholesterol by Up to 40 Percent Without Drugs or Deprivation
Robert E. Kowalski, Albert A. Kattus
HarperCollins; February, 1999

The 30-Day Total Health Makeover
Marilu Henner, Laura Morton
HarperCollins; March, 1999

The Complete Guide to Walking for Health,
Weight Loss, and Fitness
Mark Fenton
The Lyons Press; August, 2001

The Fitness Factor: Every Woman's Key to a Lifetime of Health and
Well-Being
Lisa R. Callahan
The Lyons Press; 1st edition April, 2002

The Healing Power of Vitamins, Minerals, and Herbs
Reader's Digest
Reader's Digest Adult; January, 1999

The New Encyclopedia of Vitamins, Minerals, Supplements, &
Herbs
Nicola Reavley
M Evans & Co; November, 1999

The Real Vitamin & Mineral Book
Shari Lieberman Ph.D., Nancy Pauline Bruning
Avery Penguin Putnam; February, 1997

Relationships

Chicken Soup For The Soul
Jack Canfield and Mark Victor Hansen
Health Communications

Extraordinary Relationships: A New Way of Thinking About
Human Interactions
Roberta Gilbert
John Wiley & Sons;December, 1992

Mars and Venus in the Workplace
John Gray
HarperCollins; December , 2001

Men Are from Mars, Women Are from Venus
John Gray PhD.
HarperCollins; May 1992

Men, Women and Relationships
John Gray
Harper Mass Market Paperbacks; April, 1996

Secrets about Life Every Woman Should Know
Barbara De Angelis
Warner Books; July, 2000

Secrets About Men Every Woman Should Know
Barbara De Angelis
Dell Books; March, 1991

Self Matters: Creating Your Life from the Inside Out
Phillip C. McGraw
Simon & Schuster; November, 2001

What Women Want Men To Know
Barbara De Angelis
Hyperion; August 2002

Audiotapes

Anthony Robbins' 'Powertalk!': The Six Master Steps to Change
Cassettes
Anthony Robbins
Audio Renaissance; February 1994

Goals: Setting and Achieving Them on Schedule
Zig Ziglar
Nightingale-Conant Corp; August 2002

How To Build High Self Esteem
Jack Canfield
Nightingale -Conant Corp., 1989. 800-323-5552

Make the Connection : 10 Steps to a Better Body-And a Better Life
(audio CD)
Bob Greene, Oprah Winfrey
Random House (Audio); September, 1996

The Aladdin Factor: How to Ask for and Get Everything You Want
Jack Canfield, Mark Victor Hansen
Audio Renaissance; September, 1995

Unlimited Power: The New Science of Personal Achievement
Anthony Robbins
Robbins Research International, 1986. 800-898-8669

Keep yourself alive by throwing day by day, fresh currents of thought
and emotion into the things you have come to do from habit.
— John Lancaster Spalding

Index

Goal-setting 122
Golf 154
Good fats 42, 81
Good fat nuts 84
Grains 80, 86, 93
Grandparents 93
Grape seed extract 108
Grape seed extract 108
Gray, John 147, 154
Gravitate 28, 29, 131
Green 74, 87
Green tea 74
Greeting cards 148
Groceries 16
Gum disease 85
Gym bag 67

H

Habits 3
Habitual thought patterns 8
Habit acquisition Stage 7
Habit combinations 9
Habit tips 9, 47, 61, 64, 66, 68, 78, 81, 83, 99, 101, 103, 106,
        109, 123, 135, 152
Habit triggers 9
Hamburgers 49
Happier 86, 121, 137
Harvard-based study 88
Harvard Medical School 59
Harvard University 43, 53
Harvested grains 93
HDL 43, 53, 82, 90
Headboard 30
Healthier dressing 48
Healthier teeth 73, 85

Q

R

We become what we think about, all day long..
— Emerson

About the Author

Dan Robey has spent the last 20 years studying and lecturing on health and fitness. He is the President of a consulting firm that has provided marketing communications and internet consulting services to major U.S. corporations for over 10 years. He has combined the insight gained from these studies with practical business experience to create a new program for better health, success and relationships, *The Power of Positive Habits*. Mr. Robey has been interviewed on the CBS Evening News and The Learning Channel. He lives in Miami, Florida and he is an accomplished blues guitarist.

Give the Gift of Positive Habits to your Loved Ones, Friends, and Colleagues

CHECK YOUR LOCAL BOOKSTORE OR ORDER HERE

❏   YES, I want_____copies of *The Power of Positive Habits* at $16.95 each, plus $4 shipping per book. (Florida residents please add $1.10 sales tax per book). Canadian orders must be accompanied by a postal order in U.S. Funds. Allow 15 days for delivery. My check or money order for $_____is enclosed.

Please charge my ❏   [MasterCard]   ❏   [VISA]

Please make your check payable to Abritt Publishing Group and send to P.O. Box 77-1148 Miami, Fl 33177-1148

Name _____

Organization _____

Address_____

City/State/Zip _____

Phone_____Email _____

Card#_____Exp. Date _____

Signature _____

Fax Orders: 305-675-0807 send this form.

Email Orders: orders@abritt.com

Call your credit card order toll free to:
866-MYHABITS (694-2248)